The Essential
SNOWSHOER

The Essential
SNOWSHOER

A Step-by-Step Guide

Marianne Zwosta

Ragged Mountain Press
Camden, Maine

To the memory of my sister, Carol Sottilo,
and to the memory of baby Victoria Leardi.

International Marine/
Ragged Mountain Press

A Division of The **McGraw·Hill** Companies

2 4 6 8 10 9 7 5 3

Copyright © 1998 Marianne Zwosta.

Library of Congress Cataloging-in-Publication Data
Zwosta, Marianne
    The essential snowshoer : a step-by-step guide / Marianne Zwosta.
      p.   cm.
    Includes bibliographical references and index.
    ISBN 0-07-073098-9
    1. Snowshoes and snowshoeing.   I. Title.
GV853.Z96   1997
796.92—dc21   97-19150
                                                            CIP

Questions regarding the content of this book should be addressed to:
Ragged Mountain Press, P.O. Box 220, Camden, ME 04843

Questions regarding the ordering of this book should be addressed to:
The McGraw-Hill Companies, Customer Service Department, P.O. Box 547, Blacklick, OH 43004
Retail customers: 1-800-262-4729, Bookstores: 1-800-722-4726

A portion of the profits from the sale of each Ragged Mountain Press book is donated to an environmental cause.

The Essential Snowshoer is printed on 60-pound Renew Opaque Vellum, an acid-free paper that
contains 50 percent recycled waste paper (preconsumer) and 10 percent postconsumer waste paper. ♻

Printed by Quebecor Printing, Fairfield, PA
Design by John Reinhardt
All illustrations by Maureen Kehoe, except where otherwise noted
Production by Dan Kirchoff and Mary Ann Hensel

Gore-Tex, DryLoft, and Activent are trademarks of W. L. Gore and Associates, Inc.;
MemBrain is a trademark of Marmot Mountain Ltd.;
Velcro is a registered trademark of Velcro, Inc.;
SympaTex is a registered trademark of AKZO Nobel Faser, AG;
BiPolar Technology is a registered trademark of Malden Mills;
Tiaga is a registered trademark of Tiaga.

CONTENTS

Jamie Bloomquist, Outside Images

Doug Berry, Outside Images

Doug Berry, Outside Images

Todd Powell, Outside Images

ACKNOWLEDGMENTS

Many people in the snowshoeing industry generously donated their time by reading my manuscript during various phases of its development and sharing their expertise. Special thanks go to Michael Schmidt and Kathleen Murphy at Tubbs, Jeremy Quinn at Sherpa, Russ Post at Northern Lites, Roger and Kris Dupey at Good Thunder, Bob Wallace and Marjorie Ottenberg at Polar Equipment, Lynn Cariffe and Thorn Luth at Redfeather, Jan Havlick at Havlick Snowshoes, Bill Demerest at Permagrin Snowshoes, Guy Faber at Faber Snowshoes, and Oliver Olin at Atlas. All provided excellent technical assistance.

Dick Pilsner at the Bear Paw Inn in Wisconsin, and Al Ossinger, member of the Colorado Mountain Club, contributed their expertise and perspectives, as did Paul Svetlik, member of the Colorado Mountain Club and designer of Mountain Climber snowshoes. Knox Williams, co-author of *The Avalanche Book,* contributed his time and expertise in reading sections of the manuscript. Jordan Campbell donated his time to take group pictures, as did Bob Eckhart.

Then there were countless individuals, most from companies that sell clothing and gear, who helped by answering my endless technical questions. The staff at Recreational Equipment, Inc. (REI) headquarters in Seattle was very generous with their time and photos. The REI staff in Westminster, and the Eastern Mountain Sports (EMS) staff in downtown Denver and in Westminster were very helpful. W. L. Gore and Associates provided me with excellent material describing their products. Malden Mills similarly provided excellent information on their fleece clothing.

The many students in my classes also helped. I learned much from their opinions about different snowshoe designs as we made our way through the forest on our snowshoes.

Many thanks to all. This book would not have been possible without your help. The opinions in this book, however, are solely mine. Likewise, any inaccuracies it may contain are entirely my responsibility.

Part One

About Snowshoeing

Chapter One

The Past and Present

The Pleasures of Snowshoeing

There's something magical about the mountains in winter, something that calls out and invites us to renew our spirits by communing with nature. Perhaps the call is ancestral, rooted in our distant past, summoning us to enjoy nature's pristine beauty at its winter best. Maybe the call is so compelling because contemporary life keeps so many of us tied to our desks and computers—divorced from the land. Whatever the reason, many of us long for a quiet day in the hills.

How do we answer the call and get back to the land for a brief respite? Downhill skiing is a possibility, but the slopes are often crowded, you risk injury from a fall, and the sport requires lots of skill and money. Cross-country skiing will get you into the backcountry, but it, too, has a steep learning curve and some chance of injury—at least a pulled muscle or two. Snowshoeing, however, long overlooked as a recreational pursuit by most folks, allows the average person—the nonathlete or even the senior citizen—to enjoy the beauty of winter without noisy crowds, without lots of special skills, and with little risk of injury. Why, then, has it generated so little enthusiasm until recently?

For decades, snowshoeing has had an image problem. To many people, "snowshoe" brings to mind the big, heavy, tennis-racket look-alikes, the kind that came to be associated with drudgery and fatigue, something used by mountain men long ago. This isn't an accurate picture, however. The traditional wood-frame snowshoe was superb when used on the terrain for which it was developed. But this type of terrain—low rolling hills and open plains with seemingly bottomless powder and unbroken snow—is less accessible and less pristine than it once was. Today, many of us head to the mountains to absorb nature, and traditional snowshoes have serious limitations when used for mountain travel. Because of their large size, climbing in them is difficult, and they lack maneuverability in dense forests. Let's just say that the traditional snowshoe is ill-adapted to mountainous terrain. So, during the 1950s and 1960s, the search began for a snowshoe that worked well in the mountains and thick forests many people sought out. From that search came the aluminum-frame snowshoe. It is lightweight, highly maneuverable, and perfectly adapted to use in dense forests and on steep terrain.

These modern, lightweight, aluminum-frame snowshoes have reinvented the sport. Although the first models on the market were the mountaineering variety, many folks discovered they also worked quite well even for easy, recreational walks along trails. Realizing the potential of their products, manufacturers soon began producing special models designed specifically for casual walkers who simply wanted a pleasant day in the woods. As a result, interest in the sport soared as more and more people, anxious for a day outdoors, found that these new, high-tech snowshoes are fun to use. This new generation of snowshoes opened the mountains and forests to hikers of all ages, as word spread that they could be used for anything from a leisurely meander to climbing a high peak. Runners, too, realized that these new snowshoes enabled them to continue their training runs when snow covered the ground. Soon, specially designed snowshoes were made for them, too. The result is that there are today three distinct practitioners of the sport: recreational snowshoers, backcountry enthusiasts, and runners.

The First Wood-Frame Snowshoes

Archaeologists believe that the first snow-shoes, which originated in central Asia, were bearpaw (circular) in shape. They were made with green wood that was bent into a circle, with the ends lashed together. With these primitive snowshoes, the snowshoe on each foot might be slightly different in shape and weight. To provide flotation, the frame was wrapped with strands of rawhide, pieces of vine, or strips of bark. Strips of rawhide or vine were used to lash the foot to the snow-shoe. These first snowshoes did not have a toe hole. Even in its rudimentary forms, however, the snowshoe allowed the natives to hunt during the winter, and it probably made possible the occupation of the inland areas of North America.

The subsequent development of the wood-frame snowshoe took place in North America. One of the early innovations was the crossbar, used to give the snowshoe strength. Very old bearpaw frames with a crossbar can be found in natural history museums. Later on in the snowshoe's devel-opment, early craftsmen found that the two ends of the branch could be tied together to form a long tail, giving us a frame that was a precursor of our Maine and Michigan models. The toe hole was added, which, along with the tail, allowed the snowshoe to be dragged through the snow, rather than lifted with each step. This particular characteristic, that of keeping the tail of the snowshoe on the ground, is still an impor-tant concept in snowshoe design. At some point, the concept of a raised toe entered the picture. Improved methods of attaching

the thongs to the frame were added, again bringing us closer to the contemporary wood-frame snowshoe.

At a later point in the snowshoe's evolutionary development, some tribes began using two pieces of wood, joined together at the toe and tail, to form the frame. The prior appearance of the crossbar was a necessary prerequisite for this new frame, for the crossbars were necessary to maintain the shape of the snowshoe. These snowshoes, made with two pieces of wood with crossbars, served as the precursor to our contemporary Ojibwa snowshoes. Spe-cific snowshoes for the right and left foot have also been found. Their development was enhanced by the prior development of frames made from two pieces of wood. With such an arrangement, it was easier to shape each snowshoe differently.

(from *Snowshoes: Memoirs of the American Philosophical Society,* by Daniel Sutherland Davidson, 1937)

(The contemporary snowshoer will find commercially available a fairly good assort-ment of wood-frame designs, along with several types of bindings. The frame designs currently offered, however, in no way come close to the many frame styles that were used over the centuries. In addition, contempo-rary bindings on wood-frame snowshoes, along with the footgear that contemporary snowshoers use, are very different than those used by the native North Americans. Thus, even contemporary snowshoers who select traditional wood-frame snowshoes are far from the original tradition.)

Recreational Snowshoeing

Almost anyone who can walk can become a recreational snowshoer. There's no need for formal lessons, no difficult techniques to learn, and little risk of a bad fall. Today's recreational snowshoers include families with small children, nonathletes who want nothing more than a leisurely stroll, budding mountaineers who need to hone their outdoor survival skills, and seniors looking for a way to enjoy gentle mountains and wooded trails.

Imagine walking along a softly rolling, snow-covered trail. Pillows of white top the trees, and the snow from the last storm clings stubbornly to the evergreen branches. On the ground the snow glistens like thousands of diamonds. In the forest silence, deer watch as you pass by. You come to a sunny meadow, stop for lunch, and enjoy a thermos of hot soup or tea before heading back to the trailhead. During the day you might exchange greetings with others, or you might share the silence with only the trees. Your cares and concerns have vanished into the wonderful winter landscape. You return home, pleasantly tired and ready for a restful night of sleep. Such is a day of recreational snowshoeing.

Dennis Welsh

Snowshoeing can open the door to a wealth of activities—like a hard-to-reach cross-country ski trail.

A Day on the Trail

My snowshoeing class trips always begin with a breakfast stop at a fast-food restaurant. It's an easy and pleasant way to make sure everyone is sufficiently fueled. It also gives me another opportunity to remind the group to put on *all* their clothing at the trailhead. They'll need every layer, because we'll be standing around for a while.

Once at the trailhead, we put on our boots and related footwear; then I put my entire "fleet" of 15 pairs of snowshoes at the class's disposal. After everyone is securely in the pair chosen, we're underway.

After 10 minutes on the trail, we stop to take off some of those layers: A relatively slow pace, even on a cold day, will quickly build up some heat. At the first break, as on all other breaks, we'll drink some water.

Then we'll continue on, with periodic stops to enjoy the scenery, take a few extra breaths. The scenery is always wonderful. Pillows of snow linger on the evergreens. On a sunny day, the snow crystals sparkle against a background of distant snow-covered peaks. If we are lucky enough to have a gentle snow falling, it's even more beautiful, with a quality of peace and tranquillity that's hard to find anyplace else.

Our destination is a meadow, where we will have lunch. When we stop, I advise everyone to put their insulating layers on before they get cold. On a nice day, the meadow has plenty of sun. It also has a number of camp robbers, a species of blue jay, who will join us for lunch. I can usually encourage one of these brave little feathery fellows to land on my hand by offering a tasty tidbit. If it's a nice day, and we have a leisurely lunch, many of the participants use the opportunity to trade snowshoes and go stomping around the meadow on several different pairs, experiencing firsthand the differences in performance of each design. If anyone's hands start getting cold, I encourage them to try a pair of miniheaters (hand warmers). I always keep several extra packages in my pack.

After lunch, we start back to the trailhead, with most members wearing different snowshoes than they used before lunch. Once we are underway, I hear lively conversations as people discuss the performance of different shoes. After a few minutes, we stop again to peel off the layers we put on at lunch.

When we return to the trailhead, I pile my many pairs of snowshoes back into my little car, along with the jackets and other gear that were borrowed earlier in the day. The route home takes us by a small restaurant that serves absolutely decadent pies and hot chocolate. Most members opt to make a stop. From there, we all head home, renewed and ready for another hectic week of living in contemporary society.

Backcountry Snowshoeing

Backcountry snowshoers tackle more strenuous trips, traveling greater distances into the mountains, crossing untrodden landscapes and climbing high peaks. They abandon the security of established trails to explore what lies beyond. The going is rougher, but the rewards are many: the peace, serenity, challenge, and beauty of the wilderness. Some backcountry snowshoers plan to go into the backcountry for just a day trip; others don a backpack and set out on a multi-day trip. These overnight trekkers have the added joy of seeing the sun rise and set over the winter landscape.

Some backcountry travelers use snowshoes as a means of pursuing other sports, such as ice climbing, snowboarding, telemark skiing, hunting, or ice fishing. For them, snowshoes open up whole new realms in which to enjoy their chosen activity. Snowboarders using backcountry snowshoes to get their boards into the wilderness make up a large segment of the backcountry snowshoeing population.

Although backcountry snowshoeing is a more challenging sport, requiring stamina, conditioning, and cold-weather survival skills, snowshoes are so stable and easy to use that even difficult terrain can be traveled without having to learn tricky techniques. Nevertheless, there is much to learn. Backcountry travelers must be fit, and confident in their outdoor aptitude—they must know how to select safe routes, avoid avalanches, navigate under difficult conditions, and handle medical and other emergencies.

See It, Feel It

The sometimes ferocious nature of mountain weather in the winter isn't understood until you see it—and feel it. One of the things I try to stress in the Denver snowshoeing classes I teach as a volunteer is the weather's unpredictablility. In the city, we frequently have very warm, almost spring-like winter days. But, on the same day, the weather can be much more harsh in the nearby mountains, where the elevation at the trailhead is about 5,000 or 6,000 feet higher than in the city.

When the class meets at a Denver parking lot for a trip to the mountains, I always arrive with my little subcompact almost overflowing with extra gear: down jackets and vests, Gore-Tex jackets and pants, hats, mittens, neck gaiters, and extra socks, all of which I rescued from local thrift stores. I offer each participant some of this gear, but, often, especially on days when it is mild in the city, many of the group members decline my offer, telling me that they have plenty of clothing with them.

When we arrive at the trailhead, I again offer the extra clothing. If it's snowing, which it frequently is, I watch my extra gear being whisked up and stored in the packs of the participants. When it comes to mountain weather, seeing is believing.

Todd Powell, Outside Images

More than a neighborhood stroll—a snowboarder heads for the summit.

Running and Racing

Runners who want to continue training in the winter have discovered the versatility of modern snowshoes. The desire for speed sets this hearty breed of snowshoers apart from recreationalists and backcountry snowshoers. They can run on hard-packed trails or head off into the backcountry, or they can participate in snowshoeing races, which are now held across the country.

Paris in Norway

The Sunday Telegram, Norway, Maine, Feb. 12, 1930—Norway High won over South Paris High by a score of 29 to 16 in the Winter Carnival outdoor events here in Norway this afternoon.

In the two-mile ski race, a portion of which was staged on the main street of the village, the leaders were the sons of folk born in Finland, who came to this country and settled on farms in Oxford County. The summary was as follows:

Matti Lundell of South Paris, first; Eaino Heikkinen of South Paris, second; Kenneth Aldrich of Norway, third.

The 100-yard ski race for boys was won by Lundell, Aldrich of Norway was second, and Heikkinen of South Paris was third.

Kenneth Goodwin of Norway won in the ski jump, with 24 feet and 8 inches, Harry Smith was second with 24 feet and 4 inches, and Donald Greene third. After this contest, Goodwin jumped once by himself and made 28 feet and two inches.

In the 100-yard snowshoe dash for boys, Ashton of Norway was first, Aldrich of Norway second, and Dunn of South Paris third.

The 50-yard snowshoe dash for girls was won by Alberta Hosmer, Enid Dullea was second, and Dorothy Wiles was third. All are from Norway High.

Ashton won the half-mile snowshoe dash for boys, Goodwin was second, and C. Dumas was third.

Marjorie Cummings won the 50-yard ski race for girls, and Ellen Dullea was second.

Albert A. Towne was starter of the events, and the judges were Raymond Saunders, Guy Rowe, Paul Hosman, and Edward A. Brown.

Part Two

Snowshoe Design and

Dennis Welsh

Technique

Chapter Two

Snowshoe Design

A Bit of History

The traditional snowshoe, fashioned of wood and laced with rawhide, is a venerable piece of workmanship and ancient technology. Archaeologists believe the snowshoe originated thousands of years ago, probably in Asia. Some people believe North America and Asia were bridged by land in the area that is now the Bering Strait. Some historians have suggested that aboriginal people in Asia trekked on snowshoes across this land bridge to become the first settlers of North America. After their arrival, they would have found their snowshoes to be essential for survival—without them, there would have been no way to hunt or explore during the winter. Over the centuries, the native people of North America perfected the snowshoe. Early European settlers arriving here found the Native North Americans using snowshoes, and the subtle and painstaking art of constructing them was subsequently passed on to the settlers, soon becoming a part of the culture of these newest American colonists and their progeny.

The Snowshoe Call

(Dedicated to the Montreal S.S. Club by W.G. Beers, 1874)

Here's to the slim snowshoe
In glory we renew,
Its fame will live and pleasure give
To manly hearts and true.
May its graceful dipping
The fair and brave enthral,
And with it live the echoes of
Our mountain snowshoe call.
*   Tull-lul-lul-li-it-too*

Chorus—Hear the wild shout of the
snowshoers!
*   Tull-lul-lul-li-it-too*
Ringing o'er mountain and valley!
*   Tull-lul-lul-li-it-too*
Dying away in the valley.

Here's to the rousing song
We sing as we tramp along,
Over the hill it bounds and trills
In echoes clear and strong.
If the strength and glory
Of youth you would recall,
Then exercise your lungs and limbs
On snowshoes with our call.

Chorus—Hear the wild shout of the
snowshoers!
*   Tull-lul-lul-li-it-too*
Ringing o'er mountain and valley!
*   Tull-lul-lul-li-it-too*
Dying away in the valley.

(from *The Snowshoe Book,* Second Edition, by William Osgood and Leslie Hurley, The Stephen Greene Press, Brattleboro, Vermont, 1975)

What Handling Characteristics Should a Snowshoe Have?

Consider the natural motion of the feet when walking: First the heel strikes the ground; then the foot rolls forward and the heel rises while the other foot is swinging ahead. With the next step, the cycle repeats. The snowshoes you select should allow your feet to roll through this same motion.

Next, consider the type of terrain you might encounter during a day of snowshoeing. It may be flat, hilly, or steep. You might encounter deep snow, packed trails, or ice. You might have to climb or descend steeply, or traverse (cut across) a slope. Downed timber could be strewn across the forest floor, blocking your path and forcing repeated steps over obstacles in your way.

Heavy underbrush could provide additional navigational hazards. You'll need a snowshoe that can handle all the sometimes not-so-friendly terrain you might encounter.

What type of snowshoes should you use? As you will see, no one snowshoe is perfect in all situations. Both traditional wood-frame snowshoes and the new, aluminum and synthetic varieties are designed to allow the foot to rotate normally with each step. When it comes to performance under specific conditions, however, you will find vast differences between them. The traditional snowshoe excels in deep powder on gentle terrain, while the modern snowshoe performs superbly in steep terrain.

The Traditional Wood-Frame Snowshoe

The traditional snowshoe frame is made of wood and usually has one or more crosspieces to maintain its shape. The choice of wood for the frame is very important. Many types of trees—ash, birch, and larch, among others—were used over the centuries, but the best was found to be white ash. It is lightweight and strong, and it bends easily after it's been steamed. Most designs include a long tail. Once constructed, the frame is laced with rawhide to give it flotation (ability to stay on top of the snow). One particular part of the snowshoe, the toe cord, is more heavily laced; it is here that the binding is attached. Forward of the toe cord is the toe hole. The lacing material used and the amount of toe rise a particular design has are important factors in its overall functioning.

The Pivot System

The toe cord is the pivot device that allows a snowshoer to walk normally, which on wood-frame snowshoes is achieved through the integrated action of the toe cord, binding, and toe hole. After the bindings are attached to the toe cord, enough play remains at the attachment point to allow the foot to roll forward through the toe hole with each step. This motion around the toe cord is essential. However, the play in the bindings that allows this motion has a downside: It also allows the foot to slip sideways on the toe cord. In an extreme case, your foot might be heading in one direction while your snowshoe goes in another.

The problem of keeping the foot and the snowshoe heading in the same direction was partially solved by adding a long wooden tail and providing the toe of the snowshoe with a fair amount of rise. The long and somewhat heavy tail would remain on the ground during each step forward, acting like a rudder and keeping the snowshoe moving in the same direction as the foot. This tail dragging has another benefit. Because the tail stays on the ground, the snowshoer never has to lift the the snowshoe's entire weight. The placement of the toe cord within the frame was equally important. By locating it forward of the balance point, the toe of the snowshoe

would rise out of the snow with each step. Thus, a time-tested combination emerged—wood frame with an upturned toe, long tail, toe hole, and bindings mounted on the toe cord—that enabled the foot to roll forward and the heel to rise with each step, and the snowshoe to follow the direction of the foot, or "track" well, as it glides through deep snow. It was on these well-designed snowshoes that people walked through thousands of years of American prehistory.

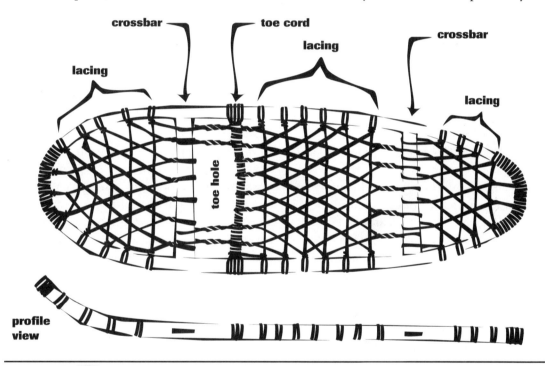

Ash Is Best

White ash is best for traditional snowshoe frames. It's strong, lightweight, and bends well after being steamed. But not every ash tree makes the grade. The tree must be knot-free and straight-grained. New York's Havlick Snowshoe Company reports that

it finds the best ash trees on north-facing slopes because these trees grow slowly and have a tight grain structure. Even with careful selection of the trees, the company notes, only 20 percent of the ash planks are suitable to be cut into strips for frames.

The Bindings

The bindings complete the integrated system that allows normal foot motion. Native North Americans used a binding that was exceedingly simple. The Attikameks—a group of Algonkian-speaking people in the area that extends from Labrador to Alberta and includes the northern United States—use such a binding. Theirs consists of two separate straps of smoke-tanned moose hide. One strap keeps the toe in place, and the second secures the heel. Once adjusted for the user, it is very easy to get in and out of. It works extremely well if you are wearing soft moccasins, standard Attikamek footgear. Many contemporary snowshoers in the far north still use this type of simple design.

Over the years, more sophisticated bindings became popular. Commercially available designs have a set of straps or laces in the toe area, a strap that goes around the heel, and usually an instep strap. All contemporary bindings are attached to the toe cord, and they keep the ball of the foot over the toe cord. The binding anchors only the toe of the boot to the snowshoe. The heel strap keeps the boot in the binding. This binding design keeps the snowshoer's foot secured to the snowshoe at the pivot point and allows the heel to rise as the foot rolls forward through the toe hole with each step. The binding is purchased separately and mounted on the snowshoe.

Frame Shape

Having established the overall mechanics of the wood-frame snowshoe, let's consider next the shape of the frame. Many frames made by the native craftsmen and the colonists who fol-lowed were designed to work well on local terrain, of which there was a prodigious variety. Naturally, many different frame shapes were developed. Most were excellent in deep snow. None of them, however, could handle all of the situations encountered in mountain travel.

Alaskan and Yukon snowshoes are long, usually between 48 and 60 inches, and have upturned toes and long wooden tails. Most are between 10 and 12 inches wide. Because of their large size, they provide superb flotation in bottomless powder. However, their length makes them a poor choice for climbing steep terrain or negotiating dense brush. Sometimes the only way up a steep slope is to kick the toe of your snowshoe into the slope and try to compress the snow underneath it into a platform from which the next step upward can be made. This technique, referred to as "kicking steps," is impossible with an Alaskan or Yukon snowshoe. In open terrain, the snowshoer could sometimes "traverse" a slope—angling back and forth, creating a platform for the snowshoes and gradually moving uphill with each step. Not surprisingly, you can't traverse with these large snowshoes in dense forests. Similarly, the length of the snowshoes makes stepping over downed timber difficult.

Maine and Michigan snowshoes, sometimes referred to as beavertail snowshoes, are not as long as the Alaskans or Yukons, and thus are more maneuverable. Most are between 40 and 48 inches long and have a slightly upturned toe and a long tail that tracks well in the snow. They are, however, a bit wider, with widths ranging from 11 to 14 inches. The Maine and Michigan snowshoes are similar, although the Maine has a more pointed toe with a bit more upturn than the Michigan. Both models are shorter and have less toe upturn than the Alaskan and Yukon models, making them more suitable for kicking steps during steep ascents. However, because they are wider than the Alaskan and Yukon snowshoes, traversing a slope in them is more difficult.

The Ojibwa snowshoe has a pointed, upturned toe and a long tail. It ranges in size from 9 by 36 inches to 12 by 60 inches. The pointed toe cuts easily through the snow and works well in brush as it moves vegetation aside. Like many other traditional snowshoes, it does not climb well but is good in deep snow.

The bearpaw, an oval snowshoe that is short and wide, is designed to be more maneuverable in dense brush. Most models have a flat toe or a toe with minimal upturn, which makes them excellent for kicking steps into the slope during a steep climb. Most are between 13 and 15 inches wide, with lengths ranging from 30 to 36 inches. Descents are difficult on bearpaws because the flat toe can easily get caught under the snow, resulting in a tumble. Traversing is also difficult because of the width of the snowshoes. Because this design lacks a long wooden tail, it does not track as well as the Alaskan, the Yukon, the Maine, the Michigan, or the Ojibwa. Nevertheless, the fact that it is more maneuverable than other models has led to a number of modifications that remedy its shortcomings. One, the Westover, adds a short tail to improve tracking. Another, the Green Mountain Bearpaw, retains the rounded, laced tail but is made a bit narrower and has an upturned toe. It has a hybrid frame, about 10 inches wide and 36 inches long, and represents an attempt to incorporate the best features of many different designs. It also tapers a bit toward the tail, facilitating the placement of the opposite shoe

when walking. This snowshoe has some climbing ability and is more maneuverable in dense brush than many of the earlier models. The Green Mountain Bearpaw is in many ways the prototype for the fully modern, aluminum-frame snowshoe.

The Lacing

In traditional snowshoes, flotation is achieved by lacing the inside of the snowshoe frame with some type of rawhide, sometimes referred to as *babiche*. The snowshoe is laced while the rawhide is moist. As the rawhide dries, it shrinks, making it very taut. To protect the frame and the rawhide from moisture, the entire snowshoe is varnished. In more recent times some manufacturers have replaced rawhide with neoprene as the lacing material. Its main advantage is that it is not affected by moisture. On the downside, it is heavier than rawhide. You will also find various types of nylon lacing used in contemporary laced snowshoes.

Traction Devices

The lacing and crossbars of traditional snowshoes provide traction as they cut into the snow with each step. Some snowshoers enhance traction by buying separate traction devices, modifying them as necessary, and then attaching them to the underside of the snowshoes.

Snowshoe Size

Traditional laced, wood-frame snowshoes tend to be larger than their aluminum-frame counterparts. Most frame designs come in different sizes, and some of the older books on snowshoeing and the manufacturers of

Wood-frame snowshoes were developed to suit local conditions—hence the variety of shapes and sizes.

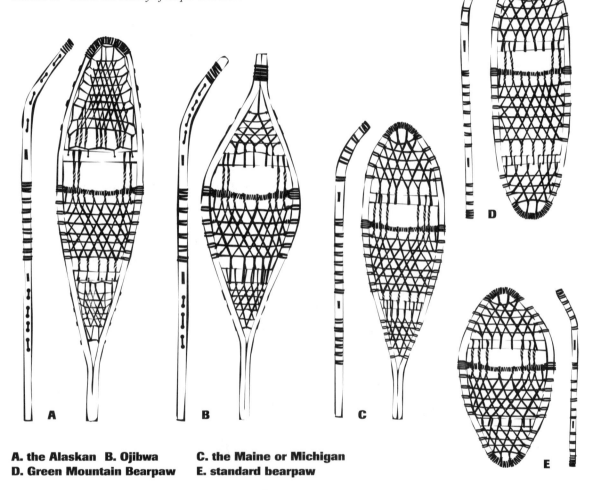

A. the Alaskan B. Ojibwa   C. the Maine or Michigan
D. Green Mountain Bearpaw   E. standard bearpaw

traditional wood-frame snowshoes have sizing charts. What size do you need? It depends on snow conditions and your weight, including gear. Snow conditions are very important. A snowshoer will sink more into dry snow than into wet snow. So larger snowshoes are better in very dry snow.

Summing It Up

Traditional wood-frame snowshoes have a binding and pivot system combination that allows normal foot motion. They excel when it comes to flotation, a function of their large size. On the downside, their size makes them difficult to maneuver, and their binding and toe cord system sometimes does not provide enough lateral control. And, they do not handle steep terrain very well.

You will find several companies manufacturing laced, wood-frame snowshoes. Appendix A provides a list of manufacturers. Wilcox and Williams, Inc., of Edina, Minnesota, sells kits from which you can make your own snowshoes, and there are also books available that teach you how to make them. See Appendix C for further information about these and other sources.

It should be noted that new technologies are being applied to traditional wood-frame snowshoes. Tubbs Snowshoe Company, in addition to offering an extensive line of aluminum-frame snowshoes, offers traditional wood-frame Green Mountain Bearpaw snowshoes onto which it has mounted its high-tech bindings and crampons (traction devices), the type used on its aluminum-frame backcountry snowshoes. This traditional snowshoe combines the beauty of finely crafted wood-frame snowshoes with the control features found on high-tech models. Faber & Company,

a Canadian manufacturer, offers wood-frame snowshoes in its Freetrail line. These snowshoes include a neoprene deck, crampons, and a unique binding and pivot system that eliminates the free play and resulting lack of control that sometimes occurs with the toe cord and binding system of traditional snowshoes. Faber also offers a Winter Hiker snowshoe, which has a co-polymer deck.

Traditional wood-frame snowshoes are still very much alive and in use, particularly in the far north in the United States and in Canada, in areas where the snow is very deep and travel does not require climbing peaks or any other maneuvers associated with mountainous terrain. One researcher studying traditional snowshoes used by native North Americans noted that when used on the terrain for which they were designed, and with the traditional moccasins and bindings, they surpass the modern, high-tech variety. Unfortunately, much of the terrain on which traditional wood-frame snowshoes excel has been paved, planted, or blacktopped, forcing many of us to search for snowshoes suited for use in the mountains, our last great haven of undeveloped land.

World's Largest Snowshoes

The Press Herald, Norway, Maine, Feb. 23, 1930—The world's largest pair of snowshoes were made for a snowclad-hills enthusiast who tips the scales at some 400 pounds.

The shoes—nearly six feet long, a foot wide, and with twice the bearing-up area of ordinary snowshoes—are patterned by Lewis D. Gibson in the Norway snowshoe factory which made both the Peary and the Byrd snowshoes from a design worked

up by a husky Eskimo in his dingy Northern Alaska snow igloo.

The factory is working overtime to build these shoes for hunters, lumbermen, and trappers after the old guides and veteran woodsmen gave the innovations a trial. The chief advantage of this new style is that the bearing value of the shoe lies back of the tail—the tail being spread out. Without widening the shoe it has a bearing-up value as great as if the shoe were 18 inches wide.

The Aluminum-Frame Snowshoe

Aluminum-frame snowshoes, originally developed in the Cascade Mountains of the Pacific Northwest, have made mountain travel a lot easier. The company that is now Sherpa Snowshoe Company began offering them in 1973. These snowshoes had an aluminum frame, a deck made of synthetic material that was laced to the frame, a metal pivot rod to serve as the toe cord, a toe hole through which the foot could rotate on the rod, superb crampons, and a very secure binding. The bindings and crampons were attached to the pivot rod, which, being metal, gave the snowshoes excellent lateral stability. Because these snowshoes were developed in the western United States, they were originally referred to as "western" snowshoes to distinguish them from the traditional wood-frame ones. Knowledge of their ability to handle steep terrain spread, and soon they were in use in the mountains in the East as well. By the early 1990s, several new companies had entered the arena, each offering its own unique variety of aluminum-frame snowshoes.

Although originally designed for climbing, aluminum-frame snowshoes were soon found to be excellent "all-terrain" snowshoes that could be used for everything from tame trails to steep, mountainous terrain. They allow the snowshoer to climb, descend, and traverse steep slopes and to navigate through dense brush and deep snow, but they also provide good traction for walking on hard-packed trails. In short, they can handle most of the situations usually encountered by snowshoers.

Continuing research and development has led to all sorts of frame shapes and bindings. A new pivot system, a flexible strap onto which the binding and traction device could be attached, was introduced in the 1980s. There are also lighter duty snowshoes, designed to meet the specific needs of recreational users who want to stay on gentle mountain trails, as well as special snowshoes for those hardy souls who use them for training runs in snow.

As you begin looking at the new generation of high-tech snowshoes, you'll notice that they do not have the long tail found on traditional wood-frame snowshoes. On aluminum-frame snowshoes, the steering control provided by the tail on wood-frame snowshoes is instead provided by improved toe cord systems and improved bindings. These components prevent lateral motion, making the snowshoe follow the forward motion of the snowshoer's foot, rather than allowing it to stray off to the side. Placement of the pivot device, too, is important in the handling of aluminum-frame snowshoes. The pivot device, either a rod or a strap, is placed in the forward part of the shoe so that the toe lifts up with each step. The overall performance of the snowshoes is influenced by the frame shape, the deck material and how it is attached to the frame, the type of pivot system, the bindings, and the traction devices. These are the basic components of snowshoe design.

The Frame

Aluminum-frame snowshoes are very strong because they are made from high-quality, lightweight aluminum. Frame shape can be either symmetrical or asymmetrical, with many varieties of each. Most of the symmetrical frame designs are adaptations of traditional wood frame designs.

Symmetrical Frames

The right and left frames of symmetrical snowshoes have the same shape. All have upturned toes. Some manufacturers use a round-tail or "bearpaw" design, borrowed from the design of the Green Mountain Bearpaw, which provides more surface area, and thus more flotation, than other symmetrical designs currently in use.

The "V-tail," or teardrop, snowshoe frame is based on the design of fine wood-frame snowshoes with long tails. The tail of the modern, aluminum-frame snowshoe, however, is very short. The tapered tail is designed not to provide directional stability, as in the wood-frame snowshoes, but to provide clearance for the toe of the other shoe when walking.

Asymmetrical Frames

Asymmetrical frames have different shapes for the right and left feet. All have upturned toes. In general, the asymmetrical shape allows the snowshoer to keep the feet closer together. Many shapes are available, including those with cutout sections in the rear. One design, made by Yuba Shoes, resembles the shape of the human foot. Asymmetrical frames are found on running, recreational, and backcountry snowshoes.

The Overall Difference

Many snowshoers feel that asymmetrical snowshoes promote a more natural stride by

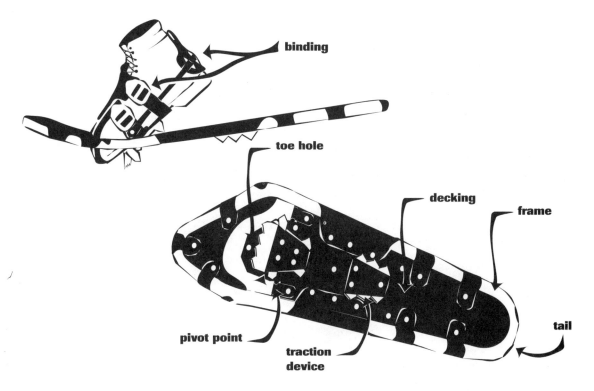

The aluminum-frame snowshoe.

allowing the feet to come closer together. This is generally true, but the improvement comes at a price. Because most are narrower or have cutout sections in the rear, asymmetrical snowshoes do allow the feet to be brought closer together; but at the same time, most have less surface area and thus less flotation than their symmetrical counterparts. Also, some feel that designs using a cutout section reduce balance in deeper snow since the snowshoe sometimes leans inward. Besides, symmetrical snowshoes won't necessarily cause you to walk or run with an unnatural stride. Widths in adult sizes usually begin at 8

inches, which is much narrower than the width of many traditional wood-frame snowshoes. If properly sized for you, symmetrical snowshoes permit you to walk comfortably and naturally.

The main advantage of asymmetrical snowshoes becomes more apparent when the snowshoes are used for running. Ankle banging can be a real problem for runners since they are moving so quickly, and asymmetrical designs tend to reduce this problem. Recently, however, uniquely shaped symmetrical frames designed to reduce this problem have been introduced. Sherpa Snowshoe Company and

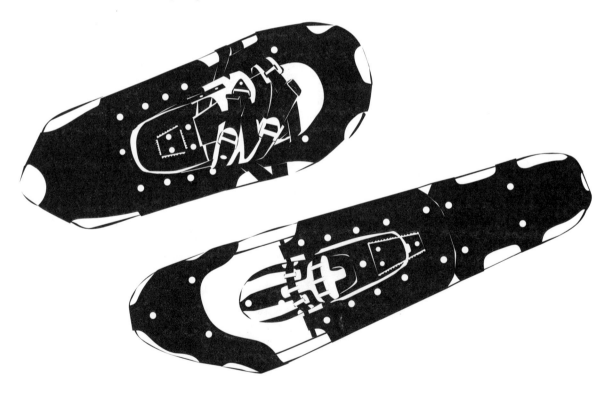

Symmetrical, top, and asymmetrical designs.

Atlas Snowshoe Company both offer symmetrical snowshoes shaped for runners. Base your decision about the best type of frame for your purposes on how the snowshoes actually feel on your feet.

The Deck

The deck is the center panel of material attached to the frame, providing the snowshoe's flotation. Traditional snowshoes, made with laced rawhide or neoprene, have many deck openings, similar to the openings in a tennis racket. Aluminum-frame snowshoes have solid decks made from materials such as Hypalon, the same material used to make inflatable rafts, or urethane-coated nylon. Because these synthetic materials are solid, they provide more flotation than laced rawhide, enabling designers of aluminum-frame snowshoes to reduce snowshoe size. We are now seeing the introduction of new solid decking materials that enable manufacturers to make lower priced snowshoes, but top-of-the-line snowshoes continue to be made with the more expensive Hypalon or urethane-coated nylon.

There are several techniques for attaching the deck material to the frame. The wraparound approach with riveting is common. The deck can also be laced to the frame. Although it might appear that the lacing represents a weak point, being susceptible to fraying, this is not the case. The two major manufacturers employing this technique, Sherpa Snowshoe Company and Tubbs Snowshoe Company, use high-quality lacing materials that have been tested for their ability to resist abrasion.

Most manufacturers now have a heel strike plate on the deck of their snowshoes. It serves two purposes. It keeps the heel of the boot from wearing the deck material, and it provides additional stability by preventing the boot from sliding on the deck surface.

The Pivot System

Like traditional snowshoes, aluminum-frame snowshoes are designed so the foot can roll from heel to toe with each step, just like it does when walking on dry ground. The pivot point around which this motion takes place is sometimes called the snowshoe's toe cord, a term borrowed from traditional designs. When the pivot process is described in reference to aluminum-frame snowshoes, the term "pivot system" is frequently used. More than any other single component, the pivot system governs how the snowshoes handle. Three systems are currently in use.

The Rotating-Pivot System

The rotating-pivot system was the only type available when the first aluminum-frame snowshoes, offered by Sherpa, appeared on the market. This pivot system consists of a metal rod onto which the binding and the traction device are attached. Like the pivot system on traditional snowshoes, the rotating pivot maintains normal foot motion by allowing the planted foot to rotate down through the toe hole as the other foot is moving forward. In fact, the entire motion of taking a step forward on snowshoes with a rotating-pivot system is similar to the process as it takes place on traditional wood-frame snowshoes.

The rotating-pivot system permits free rotation of the snowshoe's deck. When the snowshoe is lifted for the forward part of the stride, the tail of the snowshoe drops downward, rotating around the pivot rod. This is its distinguishing characteristic; the tail of the snowshoe always stays in the snow. The term "free rotation" is frequently used to describe the motion of the snowshoe's deck.

This design provides many benefits. Because the tail remains slanted down into the snow as the snowshoer takes a step, snow can slide off the deck, important in deep powder because the snowshoer won't have to lift a snowshoe deck loaded with snow. And, the stiff metal rod adds to the snowshoes' lateral stability. It eliminates the sideways movement in the binding that can be a problem with traditional wood-frame snowshoes. This increased lateral control is a particularly important asset when traversing a slope.

Rotating-pivot systems allow for the "toe-in" method of climbing, an energy-efficient way to ascend steep slopes. The snowshoe's deck always remains parallel to the slope, allowing the traction devices good purchase in the snow. Because the tail of the snowshoe drops, the toe rises and moves out of the way, permitting the traction device to bite into the snow and create a small platform as the snowshoer moves up the slope.

Snowshoes with rotating-pivot systems, however, do have some drawbacks. The tail's staying on the ground when the foot is lifted

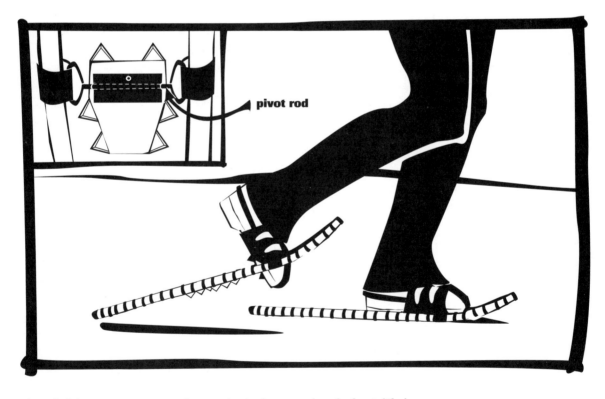

The tail of the rotating-pivot snowshoe remains in the snow when the foot is lifted.

can make it difficult to lift the snowshoes over fallen timber or to back out of tight places. Hence, they are less maneuverable. Also, having the tail stay on the ground provides no real advantage on packed trails, where getting snow to slide off the deck is not an issue.

Not all rotating-pivot designs are the same. Tubbs uses a rotating-pivot system on its backcountry models that's designed so the deck can rotate down a full 90 degrees. Sherpa, too, has a rotating-pivot system that allows the deck to drop a full 90 degrees but has reworked the design to provide "dual rotation,"(see page 27). The Yuba Shoe uses a rotating-pivot system, but it is designed to limit the rotation of the snowshoe's deck to approximately 60 degrees. Each of these approaches provides specific advantages and gives the snowshoe a unique feel.

The Fixed-Pivot System

You will find that snowshoes with a fixed-pivot system are generally easier to maneuver than those with rotating-pivot systems. A more recent innovation than the rotating pivot, the fixed pivot is a flexible strap onto which the binding and the traction device are mounted.

This system also permits normal foot motion by allowing the toe of the planted foot to rotate down through the toe hole as the other foot moves forward. That, however, is where the similarity with the rotating-pivot system ends. The fixed-pivot system greatly restricts the motion of the snowshoe's deck when the foot is lifted. The deck does not freely rotate downward; instead, when the snowshoe is lifted for the forward part of the stride, the entire snowshoe deck is lifted off the ground. Sometimes the term "fixed rotation" is used to describe the motion of the snowshoe's deck. The downward

rotation of the deck is "fixed" and limited to about 45 degrees.

Because the deck is lifted out of the snow, the snowshoe is always close to the user's foot. This is why fixed-pivot snowshoes are so maneuverable. It is easier to step over downed timber and back out of tight places if the deck is close to the boot. The fixed-pivot system is usually preferred on snowshoes designed for walking or running on packed trails. In such conditions, there is no benefit to having the snowshoe's tail stay in the snow because snow shedding is not an issue. Snow will not be falling onto the deck as it does when the snowshoer takes a step forward in deep snow. Hence, many designers of recreational models opt for more maneuverability and use a fixed-pivot system.

Many of the companies that have recently begun offering snowshoes are using fixed-pivot systems, as are some long-established companies. You will find fixed-pivot systems used on all snowshoes made by Atlas Snowshoe Company (with the exception of its economy-priced snowshoes), Redfeather Designs, Northern Lites, Good Thunder, and many others. Tubbs uses this system on its recreational and running models.

Fixed-pivot systems do have some drawbacks. Some designs kick up a lot of snow behind you, sometimes called a "rooster tail,"as the deck is picked up out of the snow during the forward part of the stride. This can coat the back of your legs and your back with snow. With some designs, a certain amount of heel slap occurs. In addition, you don't get the snow-shedding ability of those designs employing the rotating-pivot system, which keeps the tail in the snow.

You'll find lots of variability in the handling of fixed-pivot snowshoes, because the designer

The deck of a fixed-pivot snowshoe is lifted off the ground with each step.

can control performance by varying the tightness and the thickness of the pivot strap. Thus, exactly how close the deck stays to the snowshoer's foot, the amount of snow that is kicked up, and the amount of heel slap all depend on the tightness of the pivot strap, along with other factors such as the placement of the bindings, the length of the deck, and the overall way the snowshoe is balanced. A more tightly stretched pivot strap will keep the deck closer to the foot, whereas a looser one will allow the deck to drop a bit more when the foot is raised. In general, the pivot strap limits the maximum amount of deck rotation to approximately 45 degrees.

Climbing on fixed-pivot snowshoes sometimes requires a different technique than used with rotating-pivot systems. Unlike the rotating-pivot snowshoe, the tail on a fixed pivot snowshoe does not fall to the ground and clear the way for the traction device. Instead, designers count on the snowshoe's overall engineering—including its frame design and the placement of the pivot strap and traction devices. The toe rise on a fixed-pivot snowshoe does allow the traction device to bite into the snow during a climb, so steep slopes are accessible. Kicking steps into the slope to form a platform for the snowshoes is another way to climb a steep slope on a fixed-pivot snowshoe. But this technique, described on pages 48–49, consumes a lot of energy. Nonetheless, many snowshoers prefer to kick steps when climbing steep slopes because it creates a larger platform— and a fixed-pivot system makes the process

However, some designers point out that the pivot strap on backcountry models is set to allow the deck to drop away from the foot more than it does on running models, thus approximating the snow-shedding ability of rotating-pivot snowshoes.

A Dual System

Sherpa Snowshoe Company has designed a pivot system incorporating the best features of both fixed- and rotating-pivot systems. It uses a rotating-pivot rod, but it has been modified so that it allows free rotation of the snowshoe's deck in deep snow, facilitating snow shedding, but limits rotation on packed trails or amidst downed timber. The user can adjust the system for more or less deck rotation as desired.

The Bindings

Bindings on the new generation of aluminum-frame snowshoes come in many varieties, and they are the one element that changes most from year to year. As in the bindings on traditional, wood-frame snowshoes, the ball of the foot is kept over the pivot rod or strap, and the heel is free to rise with each step. A good binding must provide a reliable connection between the boot and the snowshoe; it must not allow the snowshoe to fall off repeatedly or require constant adjustment. The binding must also have lateral stability, the ability to keep your feet stable on the snowshoes as you traverse and go up- and downhill. The current trend is toward bindings that are glove- and mitten-friendly. On models designed for backcountry use, the emphasis is on maximum lateral stability.

Some bindings have toe baskets with drawstring closures, others have nylon straps across the top of the boot's toe box and instep, and

Kicking steps in a slope creates a larger platform and eases climbing.

easier because the deck is close to the foot.

As far as snow-shedding ability goes, fixed-pivot snowshoes do not shed snow in deep powder as well as rotating-pivot snowshoes.

still others have toe cages. Almost all can be used with any type of boot, although step-in bindings like those on crampons are now available on some upscale mountaineering snowshoes, requiring the snowshoer to wear special mountaineering boots. You will also find ratchet buckling systems in use on some top-of-the-line models.

Your snowshoes must track straight ahead, even if your feet don't; otherwise the frames will overlap, and you will likely go down. If you tend to walk with one or both of your feet angled inward or outward, be careful about the type of binding you use. Some can compensate for this problem better than others by allowing you to put your foot into the binding at an angle. If you do walk with your feet turned in or out, discuss it with the manufacturer or a knowledgeable salesperson to be sure that the binding on the snowshoes you're considering will work for you. Trying them on in the store and taking a few steps will answer a lot of questions.

Some bindings have a toe stop in the toe compartment. This is a good feature to have because it prevents your feet from sliding forward as you go steeply downhill.

Aluminum-frame snowshoes offer a number of traction devices.

Traction Devices

Traction devices come in many varieties and may be called crampons, talons, claws, or cleats. They are made of aluminum, stainless steel, or titanium. Configurations that provide the biting power vary with each manufacturer. Most manufacturers are now providing front and rear devices. The forward traction device, located under the ball of the foot, is the main device, and it should at least be one inch long. The rear traction device is usually a bit smaller; most are between one-half and one inch long. The forward device was designed to provide good traction for climbing.

When traversing, snowshoers need lateral traction to keep from slipping sideways, and snowshoes do not excel when it comes to lateral traction. The rear traction device was added when it was found to help the snowshoe grip the snow during traverses. It also provides better control during steep descents.

The way the deck is attached to the frame also influences traction, as does the deck material itself. Decks that are lashed to the frame provide additional traction around the perimeter of the shoe as the lacing bites into the snow. Texturing, or using a surface that adds depth on the underside of the deck also enhances traction.

Durability of Snowshoes

Your life could someday depend on your snowshoes. If you are in deep snow far from the trailhead, a broken snowshoe could be catastrophic. Thus, your snowshoes must be durable. The bindings must work, the traction devices must maintain their biting power, and the deck material must not fray or become worn easily. In short, your snowshoes must be able to take the abuse that rock and ice are known to dish up.

Manufacturers balance durability and weight so their snowshoes stand up to rough travel without fatiguing the user. Aluminum-frame snowshoes, with their synthetic decks, are durable and reliable. Most manufacturers provide a substantial warranty against broken or defective parts; some give a lifetime warranty.

Snowshoe Weight

It's often said that one pound on the feet is as tiring as five pounds on the back, and some outdoor experts claim the relationship between foot weight and fatigue is even higher. Clearly, minimizing snowshoe weight is important, and designers work hard to save ounces. A pair of superlight aluminum-frame snowshoes for runners may weigh less than 2 pounds, while heavy-duty mountaineering models may be 5 pounds or more. Recreational snowshoers can find models weighing between 2.5 and 4 pounds.

Snowshoe Size and Performance

Bigger snowshoes provide more flotation. However, the bigger they get, the heavier and less maneuverable they are. Thus, you want the smallest snowshoes that will give you adequate flotation.

Most manufacturers of aluminum-frame snowshoes offer them in three basic sizes: approximately 8 by 25 inches, 9 by 30 inches, and 10 by 36 inches.

Determining snowshoe size is an art, not a science. Body weight is a big factor. The smallest size works well for snowshoers up to about 175 pounds. The 9 by 30 size works up to about 225 pounds, and the largest size is for weight above that. When determining body weight, remember to include the weight of the gear you are likely to carry.

These size/weight categories are only guidelines. Terrain and snow conditions also affect the equation. You'll sink farther into freshly fallen, dry snow than into settled or wet snow. On packed or groomed trails, even a relatively large person can use small snowshoes, because in such conditions the snowshoes are used more for traction than for flotation. If you will be carrying your snowshoes a good part of the time, a smaller size may be a better choice.

Most manufacturers can give you precise information about the upper weight limit of each size snowshoe under varying snow conditions. If you have questions about the appropriate size, contact the manufacturer of the brand you are considering. Request a brochure and ask specific questions pertaining to your own circumstances. This should help you zero in on the correct size. The phone numbers and addresses for most manufacturers of aluminum-frame snowshoes are listed in Appendix A.

In general, small snowshoes

- allow a more natural stride
- give the best performance for climbing, traversing, and descending steep slopes
- are lighter and less tiring to use
- are more maneuverable in the woods

Remember that larger snowshoes will not entirely prevent you from sinking into deep, fluffy snow; you will simply sink less on larger ones. You will have to decide whether the added flotation is worth the increased weight of a larger shoe.

The Designer's Dilemma

The original aluminum-frame snowshoes were designed to handle all conditions associated with mountain travel, and they did this very well. They were intended to be "bombproof," and they basically were. However, they not only handled tough backcountry terrain with ease, but they also worked well on the gentle, snow-covered trails that wend their way through the mountains and forests. Soon, as more and more people began using these snowshoes for their mellow outings, a "recreational" market developed. Realizing the potential of this market, designers faced a choice. They could either continue to manufacture general-purpose snowshoes that would be suitable for all uses: recreational, backcountry, and even running on packed trails. Or, they could use unique combinations of frame shape, pivot system, bindings, and traction devices to engineer snowshoes specifically for the new-found recreational users, and they could do the same to produce special snowshoes for runners, and special snowshoes

for backcountry snowshoers. The current trend is toward specialization, especially with the larger manufacturers. And most manufacturers, regardless of whether or not they offer specialized recreational and backcountry lines, do offer specialized snowshoes for runners.

Designers who specialize can fine-tune their snowshoes to specific needs. Snowshoes built specifically for the recreational walker have lighter duty traction devices, less rigid bindings, and lighter frames, and the overall design is geared to less demanding conditions. They weigh less than backcountry snowshoes, and the price is lower. Because of the lighter weight, they are less fatiguing to use. Snowshoes designed specifically for the backcountry enthusiast have all the bells and whistles: large traction devices, heavy-duty bindings with superior lateral control, and an overall design geared to the most demanding conditions. The runner's snowshoes are super lightweight. Thus specialization has a number of benefits. It does, however, limit the terrain on which the snowshoes can be used most effectively.

In reality, there are no hard and fast boundaries between recreational snowshoeing and backcountry snowshoeing, or between any of the various domains, for that matter. Snowshoe manufacturers who offer general-purpose snowshoes reflect this fact. Recreational snowshoeing merges into backcountry snowshoeing as the trail gets steeper and the snow gets deeper. These snowshoes are suitable for recreational walks and back-country use, and occasionally even for running. You'll find that general-purpose snowshoes are similar to the backcountry models made by those companies that specialize their designs.

Injection-Molded Snowshoes

Made from a plastic copolymer, injection-molded snowshoes are the latest arrival in the snowshoeing marketplace. Like the wood-frame and aluminum-frame snowshoes that preceded them, injection-molded copolymer snowshoes have the binding, toe hole, and pivot system combination that permits normal foot motion. Several designs are available, and their uses can run the whole gamut from easy recreational trips to technical climbs. Although they are relatively new inthe United States, injection-molded snowshoes have been used in Europe for many years.

Some injection-molded snowshoes do not have a separate frame and deck. Instead, these components are combined into a molded snowshoe onto which the binding and traction device are mounted. Many different and unique bindings are in use, some with step-in capability. Just as with the aluminum-frame models, the pivot system controls the rotation of the snowshoe platform.

In the mid 1990s, Mountain Safety Research (MSR) introduced an injection-molded snowshoe called the Denali Llama. It was designed for backcountry conditions and had a pivot system that functioned like the rotating-pivot designs used on some aluminum-frame models. It also had a number of innovative features. First of all, it was modular. The basic snowshoe was 22 inches long, but either of two separately purchased flotation tails could be added. One extended the length of the snowshoe to 26 inches and the other extended it to 30 inches. These flotation tails are easily added or removed in the field. In addition to the traction device under the ball of the foot, the Denali Llamas have lateral traction rails designed to assist with traverses.

TSL snowshoes, injection-molded copoly-mer designs made in France and sold in many countries around the world, are now sold in the United States. TSL offers a number of binding options on all its snowshoes, with some bindings sporting very upscale features, like step-in capability and an easily deployed climbing arc that raises the snowshoer's heel in the binding, reducing muscle fatigue. Some of TSL's bindings allow the snowshoer to lock the heel of the boot onto the snowshoe. France's Boldas Snowshoes offers another injection-molded snowshoe that's now available in this country, and it, too, has very interesting bindings, including one with step-in capability. Boldas snowshoes have been used by French troops on the peace-keeping mission in Bosnia. Overall, snowshoes from both companies offer bindings that are very different from those typically found on snowshoes made in this country.

Redfeather Designs, a Colorado company that has offered aluminum-frame snowshoes for many years, recently added a line of injection-molded snowshoes. Its snowshoes do have a separately molded frame and deck, and Redfeather uses a binding very similar to the one it uses on its aluminum-frame snowshoes. These snowshoes are collapsible and fit into a provided carrying bag. Redfeather offers three models, with its more upscale model having a carbon-reinforced frame.

Snowshoes made from copolymer weigh about the same as aluminum-frame snowshoes. The prices of these plastic snowshoes, however, are below those of most aluminum-frame snowshoes, particularly when you compare models with specialized bindings. Prices for TSL's adult-size snowshoes begin at approximately $110, the snowshoes with step-in bindings selling for approximately $165. Redfeather's line begins at $99. MSR's snowshoe was introduced for $99, with flotation tails costing extra.

Will plastic snowshoes be accepted by the outdoor enthusiasts in this country who are accustomed to wood-frame and aluminum-frame snowshoes? Injection-molded snowshoes have done well in Europe, and these imported snowshoes have very technical bindings, indicating that they are designed and used by serious adventurers. However, many folks in this country don't believe plastic is rugged enough for more demanding snowshoeing trips. Will injection-molded snowshoes revamp the American snowshoe scene? Time will tell.

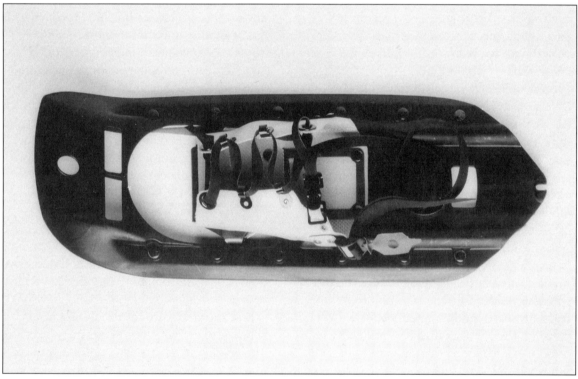

MSR Snowshoes

MSR's injection-molded Denali Llama.

Choosing a Pair of High-Tech Snowshoes

One of the biggest problems you'll have is sorting through the incredible selection of snowshoes on the market. The wide variety results from the tremendous growth of this industry and from the tailoring of designs to specific needs.

As for growth, remember that until the late 1980s many of the companies now stocking the shelves of local outdoor shops did not even exist. Until recently, the aluminum-frame snowshoe was basically a backcountry snowshoe that was used on all types of trips, from the easiest to the most technical, and for a long time, Sherpa was the only company offering one. In the late 1980s, Redfeather Designs commenced operations and during the early 1990s, the sport really took off. Atlas and several other new companies entered the market and developed very innovative designs. We began seeing asymmetrical frames. We subsequently saw the differentiation of the original aluminum-frame snowshoes into separate recreational, backcountry, and running models as the industry tried to fine-tune products for specific segments of the market. Then we witnessed the further expansion and specialization of the recreational market; many companies began offering "entry-level" snowshoes, the bare-bones ones, which cost less and are suitable for the occasional user. Likewise, the backcountry sector was further subdivided, and a high-end mountaineering variety with specialized bindings was offered in addition to the backcountry standard that had been available for years. Now, the injection-molded ones are here. All of this leads to a dizzying array of choices, but with a strategy for zeroing in on what you want you should be able to stop reeling and see clearly enough to choose the right pair.

Determining What You Want

You can do a number of things to save time and money when you are ready to go looking for your snowshoes:

- Determine your level of participation. Will you do easy recreational trips on trails that cover gentle terrain? Will you seek the added thrill of the backcountry? Are you part of that fast-paced breed of snowshoers who run? The charts on pages 37–38 show the main classifications of snowshoe use, along with the subdivisions within each. Try to pinpoint where you are in the spectrum.

- Decide what size you should use (see page 43). Remember that snow conditions should play a significant role in your choice.

- Once you define your type of participation in the sport, learn about the main features of snowshoes in that class. You already know the basic elements of snowshoe design. In subsequent chapters, you will learn how designers hone and combine these elements to produce snowshoes that are perfect for recreational trips, others that are perfect for backcountry trips, and still others that are superb for running on packed trails.

- Do some preliminary shopping just to see what your local outdoor shops offer. Most will carry snowshoes from two or three manufacturers, but they may not carry all of the models from any of them. Ask the sales staff lots of questions. Pick up each pair you are considering to see how heavy they are. Look at the pivot system to see if it is a fixed or a rotating one. Take a look at the bindings and ask how they work. Are the sales-people knowledgeable about snowshoe design and the distinguishing features of recreational, backcountry, and running snowshoes? If they were able to answer your questions adequately and help you to identify specific types, begin to make yourself a list of the snowshoes you are interested in. Try to visit more than one store, so you can get an overview of what's out there.

- If your scouting trip leaves your questions unanswered, or if you're the type who likes a broad overview of what is available, make some calls to the manufacturers to request brochures. This is also a good time to ask individual manufacturers which of their models are suitable for your specific needs. They can help you narrow your selection.

Making Your Selection

Once you've focused on your area of participation in the sport, decided what size you should get, and done some initial scouting, you need to ask yourself how much you are willing to spend. Prices change from year to year, but some ballpark figures will let you know what to expect when you go shopping for your snowshoes. Remember, however, that within each price range you will pay more for the larger size models regardless of which brand you buy. Remember also that used equipment is available to the discerning buyer at substantial savings.

Prices for aluminum-frame snowshoes begin at approximately $100, but the models in this price range are generally geared to the entry-level recreational user and the occasional user, and they carry a limited warranty.

For the occasional recreational user looking to break into the sport for minimal cost, these entry-level snowshoes represent a good value.

Recreational users wanting a few more frills and greater durability can expect to pay $140 to $200 for an aluminum-frame snowshoe. Overall, if you will be staying on trails, you will probably be happy with a recreational model. They cost less and weigh less than their backcountry counterparts. On the other hand, if you think you might want to do some backcountry exploring at some point, buy a backcountry or a general-purpose snowshoe. Or, if you just simply want to buy the backcountry model or general-purpose model for recreational trips, by all means do so. That's what most folks did before the industry presented us with this dazzling variety of specially designed recreational snowshoes.

Most aluminum-frame snowshoes suitable for off-trail backcountry exploration begin at approximately $200. Models in this range have bindings that provide superior lateral control and are suitable for use with most types of winter boots. They have aggressive crampons and will carry a substantial manufacturer's warranty, sometimes a lifetime warranty. Consistent with the trend toward increased specialization, manufacturers are now producing a special backcountry model, sometimes referred to as mountaineering, expedition, or summit snowshoes. Snowshoes in this class frequently have bindings that require a specific type of boot. If you are looking for a montaineering-quality backcountry model with specialized bindings, you can expect to pay in excess of $250. In this range you will find top-of-the-line models with ratchet-type bindings for quick entry and release. If you're looking for step-in bindings like those used on crampons, Sherpa

Dennis Welsh

provides them on its mountaineering snowshoes. Prices start above $300. When you make your purchase, make sure the binding will work with the boots you plan to wear. As you can see, if you plan to go into the backcountry, you will have to pay a bit more for your aluminum-frame snowshoes so you get the beefed-up variety that can handle difficult terrain.

Runners who plan to compete in organized races should plan to use snowshoes specifically designed for this purpose. Be prepared to spend at least $200 for an aluminum-frame snowshoe designed for running. Snowshoes designed specifically for runners are super lightweight, and the lightweight components are expensive. Most manufacturers offer a specific running model, and several use an asymmetrical frame. If you will be combining your running with some backcountry exploration, you might want to consider a general-purpose snowshoe. It will weigh more, but it will give you more options.

As already noted, injection-molded copolymer snowshoes are available for runners, recreationalists, and backcountry enthusiasts, and they are cheaper than most aluminum-frame snowshoes. TSL's adult-sized snowshoes with bindings begin at approximately $110. A pair with a very technical bindings designed for backcountry conditions will cost about $170. However, as we head into the late 1990s, aluminum-frame snowshoes are what you will mostly see in the majority of retail shops, with an incredible number of specific designs available, especially when you consider the offerings of each manufacturer. The number and variety of designs are increasing each year. And, it was the aluminum-frame snowshoe that revived interest in snowshoeing. Keep an eye on the injection-molded ones, however, because with the interest in snowshoeing we are now seeing, we can expect to see more unique and innovative designs using this technology.

Once you've defined your level of participation in the sport and have some tentative ideas as to what type of snowshoes you want and how much you are willing to spend, use the following suggestions to help you make the right choice:

- Look for a model that meshes well with your natural stride. Try symmetrical and asymmetrical designs, and fixed-pivot and rotating-pivot models. You'll find many differences in performance.

- If possible, rent a pair that you are interested in. It usually costs between $5 and $10 per day to rent them. Both Recreational Equipment, Inc. (REI) and Eastern Mountain Sports (EMS), two retailers with stores throughout the nation, rent snowshoes at many of their stores. You can also check with other outdoor shops in your area.

- If you are between sizes, try each size. Stand up on them and take a few steps. How do they feel?

- To experience the difference between two designs or two different sizes, put a different one on each foot and take a few steps.

- Don't settle for a pair that seems marginally acceptable. Dozens of models are on the market, with more being added yearly. A savvy shopper will search carefully for a pair that's just right.

- If you are interested in a model but can't find or rent a pair, call the manufacturer to see if they are sponsoring a nearby snowshoe festival or race where you can try out different models.

- If there's an outdoor club in your area, rent snowshoes and join members on a trip. You can try out a model while asking club members about the ones they're using.

If you're on a limited budget but still would like to get a top-of-the-line pair of backcountry or recreational snowshoes, ask your local shop if they will be selling off their fleet of rental snowshoes. You'll have to be patient, though. Most shops do this only once a year or so. You'll be getting an earlier year's model, but that shouldn't be a concern, because all offerings by major manufacturers during the past few years have been excellent. Get there early on the day of the sale because they go quickly! You might also check to see if your local mountain club runs any used equipment sales. These sales provide a way for members to sell off equipment they no longer need, and they help newcomers pick up equipment cheaply.

Recreational Snowshoers

Level	Price Range	Type of Snowshoe
Frequent user	$140–$200	Get top-of-the-line recreational snowshoes. Most will have a pivot system, bindings, and traction devices geared to the recreational user and will have a substantial warranty.
	$200+	You can also use a general-purpose snowshoe or a back country snowshoe.
Entry-level and occasional users	$100+	Light-duty recreational models that sport a rock-bottom price. They, too, have most of the features of recreational snowshoes.

Backcountry Snowshoers

Level	Price Range	Type of Snowshoe
Off-trail use, backpacking	$200+	Use only backcountry snowshoes or general-purpose snowshoes that the manufacturer recommends for backcountry use. They will have frames, bindings, and traction devices suitable for backcountry conditions. Most can be used with any type of winter boot.
Mountaineering and steep climbing	$250+	Get a top-of-the-line mountaineering snowshoe, sometimes called an expedition model or a summit model. Most have specialized bindings. Make sure they will work with the type of boots you plan to use.

Runners

Level	Price Range	Type of Snowshoe
On trail	$200+	Ultra-lightweight snowshoes designed specifically for running on packed trails. Most weigh less than 2 pounds per pair.
Off trail	$200+	You will need a lightweight shoe with good medial clearance that can handle deep snow. A number of companies make a snowshoe that they recommend for the off-trail runner. Refer to "Running and Racing" for additional information.

Jordan Campbell

Specialty Snowshoes

In today's competitive snowshoe market, you'll find a number of specialty snowshoes—special models for children and snowshoes that fold.

Children's Snowshoes

Anyone who can walk can snowshoe, making snowshoeing a great family activity. Recognizing this, most manufacturers are producing snowshoes to fit children. Most are suitable for body weights between 40 and 100 pounds and are designed for use on trails—the type of terrain most suitable for families with young children. The bindings accommodate shoes of different sizes, so your child should be able to use them for a few seasons. The standard 8 by 25 inch size can be used once your child reaches 100 pounds. You will find traditional wood-frame snowshoes, aluminum-frame snowshoes, and injection-molded snowshoes available for children.

Snowshoes that Fold

They are available, and they go by many names. Collapsible, compactible, folding, snap together—all describe a new type of snowshoe that can be taken apart, put in some type of stuff sack, and put in your pack until you are ready to use them. Powder Wings, offered by Wing Enterprises, have this feature, as do Elfman snowshoes, SnoTrekker snowshoes, and a line of injection-molded products introduced by Redfeather in 1997. We'll probably see more manufacturers offering this innovation in the future.

Unhinged Snowshoes

They do exist, and they don't have the toe cord and toe hole that allow the foot to roll from heel to toe. Thus, they are not good for frequent long walks. Because they tend to be inexpensive, however, they can serve as emergency gear on snowmobiles or be used by those who are looking for economy and will not be doing much walking, which is sometimes the case with activities such as birdwatching.

Chapter Three

Snowshoeing Skills

Dennis Welsh

Basic Techniques

Snowshoeing is basically an extension of walking. Because the snowshoe is stable and doesn't require much practice for proficient use, only a few steps separate the beginner from the expert snowshoer. Nevertheless, before you take those first steps, learn a few basics.

Putting on Your Snowshoes

Always read and follow the manufacturer's instructions carefully, since each has a unique binding. A number of generalities, however, do apply to most models.

Begin by identifying the right and left snowshoes. With asymmetrical designs, each is shaped differently, making the right and left ones easy to distinguish. Symmetrical frames, however, are identical. You can distinguish the right from the left by looking at the buckles on the binding's heel strap. Most manufacturers recommend that these buckles close to the outside.

Bindings have a component that secures the toe of the boot to the snowshoe and a heel strap that keeps the boot in the binding. Many have an instep strap. This arrangement allows the snowshoer's foot to lift up off the deck and rotate through the toe hole with each step. Start with the toe component. If you are using modern, high-tech snowshoes, position your foot far enough forward in the binding so the ball of your foot is over the

Binding systems secure the toe of the boot to the snowshoe and allow the foot to lift off the deck.

pivot rod or the pivot strap. If you are using traditional snowshoes, put your weight over the toe cord. In all cases, leave enough space in front of your foot so it can rotate normally through the toe hole of the snowshoe as you take a step. Then, tighten the toe component of the binding, making sure you don't tighten it so much that the binding impedes blood flow in your feet. If your binding has an instep strap, fasten that also. Next, fasten the heel strap to hold the boot securely in the binding. Then, check all closures to make sure your boots won't slip forward or sideways.

Practice putting on your snowshoes at home. It's much more pleasant mastering the details with warm hands in a cozy house than it is at a cold trailhead. Even when you've become experienced, loosen the binding straps at home so you can slip quickly into the snowshoes at the trailhead. Before leaving home, check the snowshoes for damage that could lead to problems on the trail. For traditional wood-frame snowshoes, check to make sure there are no cracks in the frame, and check the lacing to make sure that there are no worn places that might break. For aluminum-frame snowshoes that use lacing as a method of securing the deck to the frame, check to make sure this lacing has not become frayed or damaged. Both traditional wood-frame and contemporary, high-tech snowshoes are rugged, but a wise snowshoer will inspect them before each trip.

Snowshoeing versus Walking

Walking on snow with snowshoes is a bit different than walking on dry ground. First of all, you'll have the weight of the snowshoes on your feet. Plus, you'll be trekking with the additional weight of winter boots (and related footgear). Lifting these extra pounds inevitably means expending more energy.

You'll also sink a bit into the snow, especially if you are walking in powdery snow. Snowshoes don't prevent sinking; they

Long Tramp on Snow Shoes

The following we clipped from the "Gazette" (Montreal) of May 23rd 1875, which shews [sic] the necessity of early training in the use of the Snow Shoe:

"Winnipeg, May 22—E.W. Jarvis and party of the Canada Pacific Survey arrived last night. They left British Columbia last December, experienced great difficulty in crossing the Rocky Mountains, owing to the great depth of the Snow and severe weather. The Smoky River Pass, one hundred miles north of Jasper House pass, was found impracticable for a Railway nor was any other found preferable to the one already surveyed by Jasper. They traveled upwards of 900 miles on Snow Shoes, ran out of provisions shortly after leaving the mountains, but obtained sufficient game to carry them through to Edmonton. Left there April 7th, etc., etc., This is perhaps the longest tramp on record.

(from page 311, *The Montreal Snow Shoe Club*, by Hugh W. Becket, Becket Bros., Montreal, Canada, 1882. Retaining the grammar, spelling, and capitalization of the original.)

minimize it. How much you sink will be affected by the size of your snowshoes in relation to your weight, the type of snow (wet or dry), the type of snowshoes (traditional ones sink more for a given size), and whether or not the snow has been compacted by previous snowshoers, skiers, or snowmobilers.

You also can't count on consistent surface conditions. Snow is a complex substance, capable of recrystallizing and changing throughout the season in response to changing weather conditions. Conditions can vary greatly over distances of just a few feet. You may come across places where you sink, places where snow is hard-packed, and places where it's icy. Be ready to compensate, changing pace or stride or using accessory gear such as snowpoles.

Adjusting to these factors that make snowshoeing different from walking is not difficult if you are willing to make a few modifications to your usual hiking routine. For instance, don't hesitate to deviate from your usual mileage goals; as a rule, expect to cover about half the distance on snowshoes that you would cover on dry ground.

Walking on Snowshoes

Properly sized snowshoes allow you to walk normally. Snowshoes that are too large or too wide will force you to change your normal stride as you try to accommodate their extra length or width; the end result might be pain in your hip area. Most properly sized traditional wood-frame snowshoes allow for a comfortable stride. Sometimes, with the longer ones, however, it is necessary to lengthen the stride to clear the edge of the stationary snowshoe. Modern, high-tech snowshoes are narrower than traditional wood-frame ones and thus promote a natural stride. As noted earlier, asymmetrical frames, available

with aluminum-frame snowshoes, are sometimes narrower than symmetrical ones of the same size and allow the feet to be brought even closer together. Make sure the pair you select, whether it is a traditional or a high-tech one, fits well and allows you to walk comfortably.

As for aches and pains in general, you should not experience any major problems. Snowshoeing is low-impact, so it should not stress your joints. Select terrain that is suitable to your fitness level, and keep your pace slow enough that the trip is enjoyable. If you have not exercised for a while, you will probably return home tired, but it should be a pleasant type of tiredness.

Breaking trail through deep snow can be strenuous. Groups of snowshoers should share this task throughout the trip. The lead snowshoer should try to make tracks that can be used by those who follow. This is not always as easy as it sounds, because taller people go farther with one stride than shorter people do. If the lead snowshoer's tracks are too far apart, others in the group may not be able to use them. Be particularly aware of this issue if you have young children along.

You should also be aware that snowshoe design plays a major role in the ease with which you walk in deep snow. As already noted, the rotating-pivot system used with several aluminum-frame designs is energy-efficient because it keeps the tail of the snowshoe on the ground, allowing snow to slide off the deck. Traditional snowshoes also have good snow-shedding ability. They, too, are balanced so that the tail stays in the snow, and the lacing allows the powdery snow to fall through. In both cases, the snowshoer never has to lift a deck full of snow. Many fixed-pivot designs, particularly the larger sizes, are also designed to allow the deck to drop a bit toward the

Dennis Welsh

Way Back When

Wonder what snowshoeing was like back in the 1800s? Hugh Becket's *The Montreal Snowshoe Club* (Becket Brothers, 1882) preserved some history for us.

• Snowshoeing was a "manly" sport. A woman's role usually meant cheering the men on to greater efforts during the club's annual races.

• The club's weekly outings were called "tramps," usually following a route up and over a mountain at a "rattling" pace. The leader jumped over all obstacles in his path, urging those behind him to do likewise. A hotel awaited the group on the other side of the mountain, fortifying the invigorated snowshoers with bread, cheese, and ale as they sang song after song.

• The appropriate outerwear was a blanket coat with a capote (a hooded cloak) attached firmly around the waist with a sash or a belt, moccasins, and snowshoes.

• Lightweight snowshoes were available and enabled the racer to turn in better times. In December 1871, a convention of snowshoe clubs met in Montreal to regulate the weight of racing snowshoes. The decision: "That the shoes, including strings, shall not be less than 1½ pounds in weight, and shall measure not less than 10 inches gut in width."

ground, approximating the snow-shedding capability of the rotating-pivot designs.

Snowshoe design also affects the ease with which you step over downed timber or back out of tight spots. Snowshoes that have a fixed-pivot system have the advantage in these situations. Because the deck stays closer to the user's feet, they are generally more maneuverable. As already noted, maneuverability was limited with the larger traditional wood-frame snowshoes.

About Poles

Poles aid balance and provide stability in variable terrain. They help when walking through deep snow, and when ascending, descending, or traversing slopes. They provide good upper body exercise, too. In addition, poles are helpful if you should fall in deep snow. Because they add an extra measure of safety and security, use them for at least your first few trips.

There are poles designed specifically for snowshoeing. They can be adjusted to your height, and they can be adjusted to specific terrain needs. For instance, snowpoles are especially helpful when traversing a slope, since you can make the downhill pole longer. Several manufacturers offer them. LEKI makes adjustable poles that can be used with snowshoes, and their products are available

Poles can add stability and aid balance in a number of situations.

in most outdoor shops. Adjustable poles can be collapsed when not in use and stored in your pack or lashed to the outside.

You can also use nonadjustable cross-country ski poles. Pole size is not a critical issue with snowshoeing like it is with cross-country skiing, because poles are not an integral part of snowshoeing technique. Select a size that you feel comfortable with. On easier trips, you can get by without poles or you can take just a single pole. For serious backcountry ventures, you should always have either poles or an ice axe with a snow basket fitted onto it.

The Rest Step

Experienced hikers, climbers, and snowshoers use the rest step to achieve a comfortable pace and give the legs a respite between steps. The rest phase takes place as a snowshoe is moved forward for the next step. At that time, put your weight on the rear leg and relax the muscles of the forward leg. Be sure to keep the rear leg straight and the knees locked; then the bone, and not the muscle, of the rear leg will be supporting your weight.

Getting Up after You Fall Down

Even proficient snowshoers occasionally take a tumble. Hard-packed snow isn't fun to land on, but at least its firmness makes getting up easy. Falling into "bottomless" powder is another matter. In the scramble to get back up, you might wonder if you'll be there till the spring thaw! A hand from a buddy helps, but other approaches work, too. If your pack is heavy, take it off. If you have poles, plant them in the snow to use as support as you get up. You can also lay them together on the snow's surface in an X pattern to get some additional flotation. Lean on them as you try to get up. If you don't have poles, try leaning on your pack after you have taken it off.

Specialized Techniques for Traditional Wood-Frame Snowshoes

Most traditional wood-frame snowshoes, as already noted, were designed for specific terrain. Most were very large to accommodate the deep snow in the areas where they originated. Those that were large did handle deep snow very well, but they were not good for steep climbing. The snowshoer had to traverse back and forth to climb on such a snowshoe, a technique that was hardly possible in steep, wooded terrain. For steep climbing, the snowshoer would use a flat-toed snowshoe that was shorter in length and could be kicked into the snow to form steps. A snowshoe of that design, however, would not be good for traversing, and the flat toe would make a steep descent difficult under certain conditions, because the toe could catch under the snow. Thus, certain frames that were superb for one set of conditions did not always work on other terrain. Different techniques were therefore developed for use with particular frame designs. You might find specific techniques for traversing on an Alaskan, or particular methods for kicking steps with a bearpaw. These details are beyond the scope of this book—most people heading into the mountains today use high-tech snowshoes. Appendix C lists some excellent references for specific techniques to use with wood-frame snowshoes.

Specialized Techniques for Aluminum-Frame Snowshoes

Unlike wood-frame snowshoes, the new aluminum-frame and injection-molded snowshoes are "all terrain" devices. The evolution in technology that brought us the high-tech snowshoe also brought with it a simplification in technique. Modern techniques have been reduced to a few easy-to-learn procedures for ascending, descending, and traversing, and with a single exception can be used without regard to specific snowshoe designs. This exception is steep climbing, during which rotating-pivot and fixed-pivot snowshoes might require the snowshoer to use different techniques.

Caution: Not all terrain can be negotiated on snowshoes. Some slopes are too icy or steep and require crampons and an ice axe, along with knowledge of self-arrest procedures so you can stop yourself if you start sliding. If in doubt about a slope, ask yourself what would happen if you slipped. Err on the side of safety. If you are traveling in avalanche country, stay off slopes unless someone in your group who is knowledgeable about avalanche formation has evaluated the stability of the snow pack and determined that the slope will not avalanche (see page 120). Don't climb, descend, or traverse slopes until the avalanche hazard has been evaluated. Even then, there are risks. Be careful.

Ascending

How you should climb with modern, aluminum-frame snowshoes depends on snow conditions, terrain, the design of your snowshoes, and, to some extent, on your preference. If the terrain goes gently uphill, walking with your normal stride may be all that is necessary. If the snow is hard-packed, make sure that you press the traction device into the snow to get a good bite.

Steep slopes, especially those that are hard-packed, require a more aggressive approach, and it is here that snowshoe design plays a role. As noted in the last chapter, the snowshoes' pivot system is a key factor. Designs with freely rotating pivot systems, like those used by Tubbs on its backcountry and mountaineering models, allow the deck of the snowshoe to drop and remain parallel to the surface of the snow when the foot is lifted,

Climbing on fixed-pivots. Make sure the traction device gets a good bite into the slope before starting the next step.

even on very steep terrain. This clears the way for the traction device to bite, allowing what is called "toe-in" climbing. The main traction device under the ball of the foot can grip the surface of the slope like a cat's claw can grip the bark of a tree. The snowshoer can then transfer weight to this snowshoe and begin the next step upward. This climbing method is very energy-efficient.

With fixed-pivot snowshoes, the traction device's placement and the frame's toe rise clear the way for the traction device to bite into the slope. Make sure the traction device is engaged before starting the next step. Kicking steps into the slope as you climb is another approach to use with fixed-pivot

Toe-in climbing. The deck of the weight-bearing snow-shoe remains parallel to the slope.

snowshoes on very steep slopes. To kick a step, you lift your knee and position the snowshoe so that its tail is pointing up. You then kick the toe of the snowshoe into the slope and push down to compact the snow into a platform. Your steps should be far enough apart so the platform created by your new step does not collapse into the step below it. Because the deck stays close to the foot, it is not difficult to position the snowshoe with the tail pointing up. Kicking steps does, however, consume a lot of energy. Several recent magazine articles have reported that this technique is difficult on rotating-pivot snowshoes. This is true, but remember that kicking steps is not necessary with such snowshoes.

Traversing can be an alternative to climbing directly up a slope.

Be very cautious when attempting steep slopes, regardless of the type of snowshoes you are using. Heed the caution on page 47 regarding assessment of your own skill level and avalanche awareness. Steep slopes always present the risk of sliding or falling, as well as the risk of an avalanchs. Even the best snowshoes cannot compensate for a lack of expertise. Make sure you have sufficient technical skills before attempting a steep slope.

Traversing

Traversing is moving across a slope. It employs a technique called "edging" or "side-kicking." It can be an alternative to climbing directly up a steep slope; additionally, a trail you are following might cut across a slope.

When descending, keep the toe of the snowshoe up out of the snow.

You traverse a slope by creating a platform for your snowshoes. The platform is created by kicking the side of the snowshoe into the slope. Try to engage the front and rear traction devices as much as possible to increase gripping power, then press down on the snowshoe to create the platform. On soft snow, when the slope is not too steep, you can keep both snowshoes at approximately the same level on the slope by pressing down harder on the upper snowshoe to compact the snow as much as possible. On steeper slopes it is frequently necessary to create upper and lower platforms. This procedure puts lots of strain on the upper leg because it never has a chance to straighten out or relax. Adjustable snowpoles help when traversing. Make the

pole longer for the downslope side to give you greater stability. If you have only one pole or an ice axe, use it on the uphill side.

You may be able to adapt uphill procedures for traversing steep slopes, particularly if your snowshoes allow you to get a good bite into the snow without having to kick steps. Face the slope as you would if you were going uphill. Use your snowshoes' hardware to bite into the slope with each step, just as you would do if you were going steeply uphill. Instead of moving up, however, move across the slope.

Descending

Traction devices, both forward and rear, help you maintain control when descending. Both forward and rear traction devices are essential for a controlled descent. Your weight should be over your knees so that you make good use of the traction devices. Keep your heels on the deck and have enough body weight on them so the rear traction device also engages. Make sure you have a good bite into the snow before beginning the next step. If the snow is deep, keep your toes pointed up and out of the snow. Use poles for additional control. If the slope is too steep or icy, you probably should be using crampons.

If the terrain is clear of obstacles and not dangerously steep, try glissading. In this faster descent, you lean back on your snowshoes to disengage the forward traction devices. Keep the toes pointed up, out of the snow and take some long gliding steps down the slope, enjoying the exhilaration of the experience. Keep your speed under control, and don't use this technique on any slope that might avalanche—such as a hard base topped by soft snow.

Starting a glissade. Under the right conditions, it can be an exhilarating way to descend.

Traveling through Dense Brush and Heavy Timber

You are likely to come across dense brush and heavily timbered areas, especially if you climb peaks that are for the most part below treeline. You will have to step over many downed trees and maneuver through some tight areas. The qualities of fixed-pivot snowshoes become evident in such circumstances. Because the deck of a fixed-pivot snowshoe stays close to the foot, you don't have to lift your leg extra high to get the whole snowshoe over obstacles. If you are using snowshoes with a rotating-pivot system, however, you will have to raise your

leg a bit higher in order to get the snowshoe's tail to clear downed timber or other obstacles, expending significantly more energy. During a long trek under such conditions, you could become very tired on snowshoes with a rotating pivot system. Regardless of which type of snowshoes you are using, take care with each step how you plant your snowshoes. Do not use your snowshoe's deck as a bridge between two logs or rocks; this puts a lot of stress on the snowshoes and could cause some damage.

Sometimes you might need to back up or change direction as you are making your way through the forest. Snowshoes have never been known for their ability to go in reverse. Nevertheless, fixed-pivot snowshoes, especially the smaller sizes, make the task easier because the snowshoe is close to the foot. To back up, you can try lifting up the snowshoe and stepping back; or, you may be able to reverse direction by taking many tiny turning steps. With larger snowshoes, especially rotating-pivot designs, it sometimes is better to use a "kick turn" to reverse direction. To do this, lift up one snowshoe so that it is vertical; then turn it 180 degrees and plant it firmly in the snow. Next, swing the other snowshoe around and place it beside the reversed one. It's a good idea to use poles for support while you are doing this.

Putting It Together on Technique

Today's highly stable and maneuverable snowshoes give you the ability to walk in deep snow and to climb, descend, and traverse steep slopes. You need to learn only a few basic facts before donning your snow-

Back to Normal

Just ask Murphy: Sometimes when things start going awry, you can't get back to normal.

Some friends and I were backpacking in a light freezing rain on a 17-degree December day in New York state. As we began crossing what appeared to be a meadow, our lively conversation was interrupted by a loud splash. I turned to see a friend standing sheepishly in waist-deep water. Our meadow was really a swamp, and while the ice was able to support the lighter members of the crew, our heavier friend was not so fortunate.

He quickly climbed from the frigid water, and we began working on his boot laces, which had begun to freeze. Fortunately, the group had enough extra clothes to allow our swimmer to shed his wet ones.

That put an end to our hiking plans for the day, and we headed for the warmth of our cars. We had shuttled to the trailhead and had parked our now-soggy companion's car, tuned up only the week before, at the end of the trail. Things going the way they were, the car wouldn't start—of course. I was then selected to get to a phone and ask the local police for a ride to the trailhead, where the other cars were parked. Apparently I wasn't up to the task, because the police showed no interest in helping us. Luckily, a passing stranger graciously braved the icy road conditions to get us all back to our cars.

Was everyone unhappy about our turn of bad luck? Hardly. We had learned something about reading the winter landscape—and we'd armed ourselves with a story we'd be telling and laughing about for years to come. That's one of the beauties of back-country experiences.

shoes and taking off. More specialized techniques will add to your mobility in difficult terrain. Overall, a good portion of snowshoeing technique amounts to common sense. You assess the terrain awaiting you and decide how to make maximum use of your snowshoeing hardware. Make sure, however, that you also have the common sense to stay off technical terrain until you have had some training.

Maintenance and First Aid for Your Snowshoes

When you bring your snowshoes home, clean off any mud or debris that may have collected on the deck or the underside. Check the deck material or the lacing to make sure that none of it was damaged. Take a look at the bindings to see if they are wearing at any stress points. Make sure the snowshoes are ready for your next outing before you put them away.

Traditional wood-frame snowshoes do require regular maintenance. The frames should be varnished at least once per season. Many veteran snowshoers recommend using a spar varnish. If the lacing is rawhide, it, too, must be varnished. Wet rawhide sags, so it has to be protected. This is why it is important to inspect your snowshoes every time you return home. If any of the varnish has worn away, you will need to touch them up and allow time for the varnish to dry. Don't use the snowshoes until the varnish has completely dried, following the directions on the can for drying time. Some seasoned snowshoers recommend giving the varnish an additional day or so to further cure. When neoprene lacing is used, the neoprene should not be varnished; nevertheless, the frame must still be varnished as needed. Store your wood-frame snowshoes in a cool, dry place, and if they are laced with rawhide, keep them away from hungry rodents looking for something to gnaw.

Aluminum-frame snowshoes, however, are virtually maintenance free. That does not mean you should not be kind to them. Let them dry completely, and then store them in a dry place away from direct sunlight. The synthetic materials used in contemporary snowshoes will not be damaged easily by either moisture or sunlight, but over a long period of time these elements will take their toll. With a little good care, your snowshoes will continue to look good and function perfectly for many years.

What do you do if a snowshoe breaks in the backcountry? Wood-frame snowshoes can be splinted just as you splint a broken bone. The references on traditional snowshoes at the end of the previous chapter ("Snowshoe Design") provide detailed instructions on making repairs to both the frame and the lacing. What, however, do you do if your aluminum-frame snowshoe breaks? Fortunately, broken frames are not common on these snowshoes. Bindings, though, have been known to break. Always carry a repair kit of your own devising: duct tape and nylon parachute cord. Your own ingenuity will provide the best solution. It's also wise to avoid doing the types of things that are hardest on snowshoes, such as using them to form a bridge between two rocks or logs.

Part Three

Recreational Skills

Chapter Four

Planning and Preparing for a Recreational Trip

Recreational snowshoers enjoy the winter landscape in a leisurely way. They like gentle terrain, they often stay on trails, and they avoid extreme weather. They seek a pleasant day's wandering through the snow-covered forests and mountains. While it's a great activity for families, seniors, and others who don't want too much strain, recreational snowshoeing is also the best way for the more adventurous to learn the basics before heading into the challenging terrain of the backcountry. Regardless of the type of trip you have in mind, creating a trip plan and preparing yourself a bit for both the inevitable and the possible will help ensure that your trip is fun—and safe.

Trip Planning

Don't think of trip planning as a burden—it's part of the fun. Planning consists of selecting a place to go, picking a route, finding maps that cover the area, and arranging for companions. Selecting the food, equipment, and proper clothing that you will need is covered in the next chapter, "Equipping Yourself for a Recreational Outing."

Places to Go

To locate areas suitable for your first snowshoeing trip, look for guidebooks on snowshoeing trails or hiking trails in your area. These usually give mileage and the elevation gain. Elevation gain is important; unless you eat rattlesnakes for breakfast and bend iron bars for fun, your first few trips should cross gentle terrain. You might also use some favorite summer trails for your outing. Or, you can check books describing ski-touring trails, many of which are also suitable for snowshoeing.

Maps and Navigation

U.S. Geological Survey topographic maps, particularly the 7.5-minute quads (maps that cover a quadrangle 7.5 minutes of longitude high by 7.5 minutes of longitude wide), are among the most useful for snowshoers. Using them effectively, however, requires a little practice. The map's contour lines show elevation changes, allowing you to determine the total elevation gain of the intended route. Contour lines also show steep slopes that may

Keep Your Map Dry

Keeping your map in a clear plastic case will help protect it from damage. But what happens when you need to get it out in a snowstorm to refold it or take a closer look at something? Try coating the map with something to make it water-resistant, such as Aquaseal Map Seal from Trondak, Inc. Available in many outdoor shops, a small bottle of Aquaseal costs around $4 and can coat three or four topographic maps. Just dab it on both sides and let it cure.

John Lerer

present avalanche danger. Most importantly, topographic maps can be used in conjunction with an orienteering compass to pinpoint your location. If you are going above treeline or traveling off trails or in areas where wind-blown snow can quickly cover your tracks, you must be able to navigate with a map and compass. Several excellent books on wilderness navigation are available. You will find a few references in Appendix C. Until you become proficient in finding your way with a map and compass, limit your trips to well-marked trails below treeline.

Unfortunately, topographic maps are not updated very often. An old building on the map may be gone. Trails may be overgrown or may have been rerouted. And, unless blazed with markers high up on the trees, trails can be difficult to follow when covered with snow. Above timberline, trails are sometimes marked with cairns—piles of rocks—but these, too, can be obscured by drifting snow. And, trails are often not well maintained in winter. Signs marking intersections

may be missing, downed timber may obscure the trail, and foot bridges may have collapsed under the weight of the snow.

At national or large state parks, trail maps are often available at the visitors centers. National forest maps are often obtainable from the local ranger station or a nearby sporting goods store. These maps show not only trails, but also access roads to the trailheads. However, they do not usually have elevation contours or other detailed topographic information.

A new navigational aid, a Global Positioning System (GPS) receiver, is now available and can be used in conjunction with a map and compass. More will be said about this in the chapter called "Backcountry Snowshoeing."

Finding Companions

Don't go alone. Have at least one companion on an easy recreational trip, and have at least four people in the group for more challenging trips. That way, if someone is hurt, one person can stay with the victim and two can go for help. No one is left alone, and no one is traveling alone.

Finding compatible companions is important. Friendships have been formed—and lost—on outings. The group members should have comparable gear and similar fitness and skill levels, and they should share the same attitude toward the impor-

tance of reaching the trip destination.

Several factors can affect compatibility. Those who exercise regularly will be able to travel faster than those who don't. Younger children will require a slower pace. Agree beforehand on the trip's pace; it should be that of the slowest group member. Forcing slower people to keep up with the tigers risks

Fun with Fido

It seems that dogs, too, enjoy a day in the mountains and forests. Before you decide to take your pet along, ask yourself a few questions.

Is your dog fit enough to enjoy a day on the trail? If she's old, arthritic, or overweight, or is relatively inactive most of the day, you'll have do get her into shape before you can think about an outing. Dogs lack the human capacity for complaining and will follow you well after they should have stopped.

Can your dog handle cold winter temperatures? Some breeds can't. Check with your veterinarian.

Once you decide that your dog is ready, bring along gear to make her day pleasant and enjoyable. Remember that she'll need more calories trekking with you than on a sedentary day. Bring water and a bowl, and offer water frequently throughout the day. Some breeds might need a doggie sweater or coat; check with your vet. You also might need a pair of booties to prevent painful ice balls from forming on the dog's toes. Also bring a doggie first-aid kit and know how to deal with the problems your canine friend may develop. Wolf Packs, Inc.,

of Ashland, OR (phone 541-482-7669, fax 541-482-SNOW), offers booties, collapsible water bowls, and other gear for your dog.

For more information on acclimating your dog to the outdoors, check these books:

Dog First-Aid by Randy Acker D.V.M., with Jim Fergus (Gateway, MT: Wilderness Adventures Press, 1994). This small manual will fit nicely in your pack.

Happy Trails for You and Your Dog by Gary Hoffman (Riverside, CA: Insight Out Publications, 1996). An excellent guide to training your dog to be a good trail companion, with information on first-aid equipment and specialized subjects like stream crossings and boulder fields.

On the Trail with Your Canine Companion by Cheryl S. Smith. (New York: Howell Book House, 1996). Covers the broad spectrum of topics related to enjoying the outdoors with your dog, including what to pack; getting your dog safely to the trailhead in your vehicle; animal and weather hazards along the trail; the canine senses of sight, sound, and smell; and many other relevant topics.

exhausting them, setting the stage for potentially life-threatening problems in the backcountry.

Any member of the group who is not properly clothed and equipped for a winter outing endangers the entire group. Make sure everyone understands the nature of the trip beforehand, and double-check everybody's equipment before setting out.

Outdoor clubs are an excellent way to meet people who like snowshoeing and other outdoor sports. Hiking clubs are found all over North America (see Appendix B), and many of them run snowshoeing trips ranging from easy walks to strenuous treks. Find a trip that matches your ability and interest, and enjoy this pleasant way of making new friends.

What to Bring Along

Carry extra clothing, food, and water in a pack (see page 82). Plan to have lunch, preferably something hot that is kept warm in a thermos.

Following the Blue Diamond

Colorado's Rabbit Ears Pass is a paradise of deep snow, flocked trees, and winding, open meadows. There are several well-marked trails on the pass, but beware of "loops" that cross each other. Many are without names, numbers, or symbols. Getting on the wrong loop can extend your day beyond your capabilities. It happened to us.

A friend and I started out breaking trail on snowshoes in deep snow along with some cross-country skiers. Later, the skiers picked up the pace and set out on their own. We were following tracks most of the time, but some seemed to be leading off in other directions. It was snowing moderately with an intermittent wind, and at times the long-distance visibility was not good. We lost contact with the skiers and wondered if the tracks we followed were just attempts at downhill fun runs. Were these tracks to be trusted? Were we going in the right direction? With these feelings nagging at us, we pulled out our compasses and confirmed that we were going much too far north. By now we should have been going on the south loop, but we had seen no signs or symbols for some time.

We had to make a decision. Was this the wrong loop or another loop not on the map? With the possibility of a long delay of three or more hours out, and with colder and more threatening weather coming, we made the decision to turn around and backtrack. At least we knew where we had been, and turning around was safer than a survival night out. Even though we had good equipment, food, and water, we could have gone to exhaustion or gotten lost, or the wind and snow could have obscured the trail in front as well as behind us. We now felt comfortable in turning back. Years of experience and listening to our gut feelings had supported us again.

Hours later, back at our original starting place, we were relieved at the sight of other skiers and snowshoers. We knew we could always come back and try again. Later, our best reward was the soak in the hot springs down the road.

Judy Childers

Be Prepared

Preparing for a recreational outing involves being aware of potential hazards and taking the necessary precautions. It also involves being aware of the inevitable needs and limitations of your particular group and learning a few strategies to keep everybody comfortable and happy.

Dangers on the Trail

As beautiful as they are, mountains and forests can be unforgiving, especially in the winter. Snowshoers face avalanche hazards, stream crossings, and frozen lakes and marshes. Identify potential hazards beforehand by carefully studying your maps and, if possible, talking with others who know the area. These travel hazards are discussed in more detail in the chapter entitled "Playing It Safe."

Before you head into the backcountry, let a friend know where you are going, how long you expect to be out, how many are in your party, and how long overdue you can be before your friend calls the police. If you are trekking in a state or federal park or forest, check in with the nearest ranger station and leave a written itinerary.

Watch out for skiers. Snowshoers and cross-country skiers frequently use the same trails, and descending skiers often are moving fast. Be prepared to step to the side of the trail quickly to allow a skier to pass.

Trailhead Concerns

Should you stash your cash in the car or take it along? Since trailhead parking areas may be temptations for thieves, consider putting cash and credit cards in the bottom of your pack or in a pocket that you will not frequently open.

The car key is another item that requires precautions. Keep an extra key taped to the inside bottom of your pack or in that infrequently opened pocket where you stored your cash. You will also find that some packs have a special clip for attaching your keys. At any rate, don't store valuable items or keys in pants or jacket pockets; if you take a tumble, they are likely to fall out and disappear quietly into the snow.

Make sure that your car is equipped for winter conditions. As a minimum, keep a snow shovel, chains, and a tow rope in the trunk. Extra clothing is also a good idea. If you have an extra sleeping bag, keep it, too, in the trunk, ready for emergency use if you can't get your car started and you have to wait for help. Extra food and a thermos of tea or coffee to enjoy before heading home are additional items that you should consider having in your car.

Pacing Yourself

Travel at a comfortable pace, not just for enjoyment but for safety as well. Traveling too fast will exhaust slower members, leaving them without energy reserves and setting the stage for hypothermia, a deadly condition in which the body loses heat faster than it can produce it (see page 17).

As a rule of thumb, keep the pace slow enough that you can carry on a conversation without difficulty. If the route goes steeply uphill, slow down. Don't forget to stop occasionally to look around and enjoy the view. You will find that many brief stops, just long enough to take a few breaths, are more helpful than infrequent long rests.

Words of Wisdom

- Skiers' tracks aren't always on true trails—they may be "downhill" opportunities.
- Have good equipment with you.
- Keep up your map-and-compass skills and understand changing weather.

- Follow your experience, intuition, and gut feelings.
- Err on the side of safety by turning around rather than risking exhaustion, confusion, and an unprepared night out.

Judy Childers

Along the Trail

When out on a recreational trip, plan to

- Keep your water bottle handy and stop frequently to drink. Cold air is very dry. You lose moisture with each breath you take as your body humidifies the air before it goes into your lungs. Perspiration drains still more moisture from your body. Unfortunately, the sensation of thirst lags far behind the need for water, so drink even if you don't feel thirsty.

- Snack frequently. The body needs lots of energy for snowshoeing. Complex carbohydrates make excellent snacks—try peanut butter sandwiched between crackers, or nut and dried fruit mixes. Avoid candy bars that are hard at room temperatures—they'll be impossible to eat after they get cold. Keep snacks handy so you don't have to dig through your gear to find them.

- Stop for lunch. If possible, find a sunny place out of the wind. Put on extra clothing as soon as you stop. If it's very cold, stop only long enough to eat and drink.

- Remember to adjust your clothing to meet varying conditions over the course of the day. For instance, when you get hot going uphill, shed some clothing.

Before crossing windswept areas, add a windproof shell.

- Keep an eye on the weather. In the mountains storms can move in quickly. Be prepared to retreat quickly if a storm threatens. Stay aware of the time. Days are short in the winter—plan to return to the trailhead well before dark.

- Stay together as a group. Too many wilderness tragedies have begun when one member of a group wandered off alone. Other members may not know whether the missing member headed back to the trailhead by a different route or got into trouble farther ahead of the group.

Taking Along Children

Snowshoeing is a great way to introduce kids to the mountains and forests. However, you do need to structure trips differently if you want the little folks to have a good time. First of all, you will need to keep down the mileage. One relatively level mile out and back will probably be about as far as you want to go, and less than that if the children are very young. In fact, for your first trip you can stay relatively close to the trailhead while you give these new little

Dennis Welsh

snowshoers a chance to get a feel for the snowshoes without tiring them out. Remember that you want the children to have a pleasant experience.

Since most children don't relish walking just for the sake of getting some exercise, plan some additional activities for them to enjoy. You can build a campfire at lunchtime, if fires are permitted in the area you are visiting, and all toast marshmallows. You can bring a sled for a little excitement along the way; the sled can also serve as "emergency" equipment in case one of the kids gets tired. While on the trail, you can do some bird and tree identification, or perhaps identify animal tracks. You can also introduce them to the use of a map

and compass. A hot-chocolate break could fend off a chill or work wonders on flagging energy and moods.

If you're taking a group of children, make sure you have enough adults to provide effective supervision. Check to make sure that each child has gear appropriate for the outing. Plan to keep the group together and make sure that everyone understands the dangers of wandering off. Also plan on making many stops throughout the day. Encourage children to shed and add layers as necessary, and to drink lots of water. Make sure, too, that the kids are able to walk normally on their snowshoes. To complete the trip, stop for a snack and some hot chocolate on the way home.

Chapter Five

Equipping Yourself for a Recreational Outing

What Gear Do You Need?

In this chapter we'll look at the type of snowshoes you will need for a recreational outing. You'll also learn about packs and what to put in them. Many newcomers to snowshoeing, especially those interested in the more leisurely and mellow type of experience, are surprised to learn they'll have to carry some gear; but doing so is essential for safety. And then there's the matter of what you should wear.

First—the snowshoes. Recreational snowshoers can choose from a wide variety of snowshoes suitable for easy outings. Traditional wood-frame snowshoes can be used for outings that take place in deep snow on level or gently rolling terrain—the conditions for which these snowshoes were designed. Within the last few years, manufacturers of aluminum-frame snowshoes have taken a look at the specific needs of the trail walker and have put together the bindings, pivot system, deck material, and traction devices that produce in combination snowshoes especially geared to those needs. Because the recreational market is now such a large and fast-growing sector of the sport, you'll find a huge assortment of aluminum-frame snowshoes designed to meet your trail-walking needs. Injection-molded plastic ones are also available. We'll begin by taking an in-depth look at the aluminum-frame snowshoes specifically designed for recreational outings.

The Aluminum-Frame Recreational Snowshoe

When you begin shopping for your snowshoes, it's important to recognize the terminology used to identify the snowshoes designed for easy trail walking. Some manufacturers do call them their "recreational" model, but others refer to them as their "walking" model.

Frame Design and Frame Size

You will find both symmetrical and asymmetrical snowshoes designed for recreational trips, but symmetrical models are more common. As far as size goes, most companies offer at least two, the 8 by 25 inch and the 9 by 30 inch. Flotation is not a big issue with recreational walkers because they will be on packed or broken trails, not in the "bottomless" powder of the backcountry. Therefore, if you are between sizes, the smaller frame may be the better choice. It will be lighter in weight and easier to maneuver.

The Pivot System

Most winter walkers like to have the snowshoe deck close to their feet. Thus, most manufacturers put a fixed-pivot system on their recreational snowshoes. This feature makes the snowshoe very maneuverable as the snowshoe deck follows the motion of the foot. And since recreational users will not be seeking out the deep snow or steep terrain of the backcountry, most of the advantages of a rotating-pivot system, such as its ability to shed snow or permit "toe in" climbing, will not be put to use on a recreational outing. Those manufacturers that do use a rotating-pivot system on their recreational snowshoes usually engineer it so that it is more adaptable to a recreational setting. Sherpa's dual rotation is an example. It provides fixed-pivot characteristics on packed trails.

The Bindings

Recreational users do not need the same degree of lateral stability that is essential in the backcountry. Therefore, most recreational snowshoes have simple bindings, frequently a series of three straps—one over the toes, another over the instep, and a third around the heel. Other configurations are out there, but most are simple to use. They are easy to fasten, very secure, and they provide sufficient lateral stability for a recreational setting. The enhanced lateral stability provided by the more upscale bindings is just not necessary. And by keeping the binding simple, manufacturers can reduce the weight of their snowshoe, since the more upscale bindings usually have more hardware and consequently weigh more. You will also find that insulated bindings are available from some manufacturers on the snowshoes they offer for recreational users.

Traction Devices

Traction is always essential, especially on hard-packed trails in high-use areas. The traction devices used on recreational snowshoes are frequently scaled-down versions of the beefier ones necessary in the backcountry. Actually, the smaller traction devices can be a real asset on packed snow because the snowshoer does not have to lift the snowshoe quite as high to provide clearance for the device. Also, a smaller device weighs less and helps keep the overall weight of the snowshoes down.

The Deck

Hypalon and urethane-coated nylon are the primary deck material choices for use with aluminum-frame snowshoes, although newer

An easy-to-use three-strap binding.

and less costly materials are now used on introductory-level models. The wrap-around and rivet technique for attaching the deck to the frame is frequently used, since the recreational snowshoer does not need the additional traction around the perimeter that the lacing method provides.

Snowshoes for the Occasional User

Many manufacturers of aluminum-frame snowshoes are now offering an entry-level snowshoe for the occasional user. This is a more recent addition to the marketplace, and it no doubt represents an awareness of the diversity within the recreational sector of the sport. Snowshoes in this category usually have a rock-bottom price and are made of less costly materials than top-of-the-line recreational snowshoes. These low-priced models have most of the features of other aluminum-frame snowshoes—decks made from solid material, easy-to-use bindings, and traction devices—but generally they will not carry the same warranty as the higher priced models. They are very suitable for the recreational user on a budget who is looking for a low-cost option.

Other Options

For those who like "bombproof" snowshoes, there's nothing wrong with buying a backcountry snowshoe or a general-purpose snowshoe to use on recreational outings. As already noted, before the introduction of specific recreational snowshoes, winter walkers used backcountry models for their easy treks.

Injection-Molded Plastic Snowshoes

Although the marketplace is dominated by aluminum-frame snowshoes, injection-molded plastic snowshoes suitable for a recreational outing are available. Because injection-molded snowshoes cost less, we will probably see more of them geared to the recreational market in the future.

Add Some Warmth

"Cold hands, warm heart" might be a nice turn of phrase, but odds are most people will prefer the warm hands. There are a number of pocket-size, or smaller, heaters available today—one-time disposables, fluid- or solid-fueled, and even some that you can recharge by dropping in boiling water.

The disposable pocket heaters sold by Grabber are convenient, soft, and pliable. Just put them in your mittens for a few minutes or stuff them into the nooks and crannies of a pocket.

Or try a reusable heater, such as those that burn lighter fluid or something similar. One brand, the Jon e Warmer, uses a platinum catalyst heating element that consumes the fluid without a flame. The device does require lighting a wick, best done away from wind and drafts. Once going, the Jon e Warmer provides heat for about eight to 12 hours.

Heaters that burn solid-fuel sticks are easy to start and work about six to eight hours. You'll find them in many outdoor equipment catalogs.

Other reusable hand warmers are charged simply by boiling them in water for 10 minutes. When you're ready to use one on the trail, bend the metal disk inside to activate the heating device. You get about an hour's warmth. When you get home, recharge it again by boiling, and it's ready for another trip.

Boots, Socks, and Gaiters

Nothing will spoil a day faster than cold feet. If you plan carefully, however, you should not have to suffer this affliction. A large assortment of boots, socks, gaiters (leg coverings that reach from the instep to above the ankle or to mid-calf or knee), and toe warmers are available to keep your feet warm.

Boots

Remember, one pound on the foot is as fatiguing as five pounds on the back. With that in mind, look for the lightest weight footgear that will meet your needs.

If you plan to do easy trips in moderate weather, you can get by with three-season hiking boots. You can extend their temperature range with high-tech or wool socks, toe warmers, insulated bindings, and gaiters. A note of caution, however: Use this type of boot only if it has a waterproof/breathable liner or has been waterproofed with one of the excellent waterproofing products available. Don't chance letting your feet get wet in the winter. Wet feet make you more vulnerable to frostbite.

The next step up is a leather boot lined with Thinsulate or some other insulating product. Lightweight, lined leather boots may not keep your feet warm in subzero temperatures, but they will work well on moderate winter days. Their warmth, too, can be increased with the accessories described later in this chapter.

Another option is a pair of mukluks, the traditional footgear of indigenous North

Marc Muench, Tony Stone Images

Mukluks, traditional gear of Native North Americans, are lightweight and warm.

Americans. Mukluks are a soft, moccasin-type footwear made of moose hide and worn with a thick, insulating liner and heavy socks. They are known for being comfortable, warm, and very lightweight. You can use either handmade or commercially made ones. Unfortunately, you probably will not find either type in your local shops; they are available through mail order. Because the mukluk is very soft, finding a comfortable fit even when ordering through the mail is not difficult. See Appendix A for more information on obtaining each type. Handmade mukluks generally should be worn only in extremely cold weather, because they cannot handle wet conditions. Some makers recommend using them only at temperatures of 10 degrees Fahrenheit or below. If you would like to try commercially made mukluks, you can order them from Steger Designs (see Appendix A). This company has added a very flexible rubber sole to its mukluks to make them more suitable for contemporary wear. They can be used as long as the temperature is below freezing. If you decide to use mukluks, remember that they are not suitable for walking through wet or slushy snow or for hiking on dry ground into the area where you'll begin snowshoeing. You will find additional information on the suitability of mukluks for various types of outings in the next chapter, "Backcountry Snowshoeing."

Boots designed specifically with the snow-shoer in mind were a long time in coming, but they are now making their way into the market. Tiaga introduced a boot based on the thermals and traction of a dog's paw. They have fleece uppers and a felt-like fabric with good gripping power for the sole, and they weigh only one pound apiece. They are for very cold weather and should be used with the same cautions that apply to mukluks. For more techni-

cal terrain, Technica's Snow Paw is available. Technica worked closely with Tubbs Snowshoe Company to produce this backcountry-quality boot. A pair weighs less than 3 pounds. You will find more information on these boots, too, in the "Backcountry Snowshoeing" chapter.

Socks

Sock design has almost become a science. Highly specialized socks may cost $40 or more a pair. These top-of-the-line varieties usually have a layer of Gore-Tex or some other high-tech fabric to keep the feet dry. You don't necessarily have to buy the most expensive socks, however. Moderately priced models work well.

Traditionally, outdoor enthusiasts have worn two layers of socks in hiking boots and winter boots. Since your feet are likely to sweat, the inner layer, or the liner sock, should be a fabric that wicks moisture away from the feet. Don't use cotton socks, which absorb moisture and chill the feet. The out-side layer should insulate. Wool, used for generations, does a good job. You will now find synthetics made of fleece and other engineered fabrics, and these, too, can be used as the outer layer. Yet another outer layer option is a sock made of closed-cell foam. In addition, there are some varieties of socks that incorporate the wicking liner sock and the insulating layer into a single pair. As you have probably guessed, all of this means there is no shortage when it comes to sock selection.

Don't buy socks that are so bulky they will make your boots too tight. Tight boots reduce blood circulation and guarantee cold feet; in severe conditions, they can lead to frostbite. If you will be buying new boots, try them on with the socks you plan to wear.

Gaiters

Gaiters help seal the snow out of the tops of your boots, and they add warmth by providing another layer around the boot tops. Either elastic or an adjustable strap at the top keeps them from sliding down. Some varieties extend up to the knee, while others cover only the top of the boot and the ankle. The low style meets the basic requirements, while the high one adds insulation to your legs. Gaiters made of Gore-Tex or some other waterproof/breathable fabric are a real plus in wet climates.

Gaiters add warmth and keep snow out of your boots.

When selecting gaiters, consider how easy they are to put on. Front-opening models are easier to use, and Velcro closures are convenient. Before buying a pair, try putting them on in the store, and compare different brands until you find a pair that meets your needs.

Toe Warmers

Grabber Mycoal's single-use toe warmers are inexpensive and they work well. Each package contains a thin pair of heaters, shaped somewhat like the front of the foot. They activate as soon as the pack is opened. Each heater has an adhesive strip that helps keep it in place. Attach them to the outside of your socks under your toes and the balls of your feet. Toe warmers are very thin, so you won't feel them in your boots, especially if you are wearing two layers of socks. They last about five hours and produce an average heat of 100 degrees Fahrenheit. The additional heat provides just enough to compensate for the heat that is lost through conduction to the cold ground below your boots.

Insulated Snowshoe Bindings

Many aluminum-frame snowshoes designed for recreational use come with insulated bindings to provide an additional defense against cold air, thus extending the comfort range of boots. Although designs vary, most include a layer of neoprene that covers the front of the boots. Sherpa offers them, as does Good Thunder. Redfeather offers both its insulated Insulux binding and an insulated toe cover that fits over its standard binding. Probably other companies will offer insulated bindings in the future.

Keep Your Boots Warm

Some snowshoers prefer to put their boots on when they arrive at the trailhead, and for many good reasons. Heavy footwear can be cumbersome to drive in and can cause the feet to sweat, creating a moisture problem before the trip even begins. In addition, if you will be using toe warmers, you won't want to activate them until you are ready to start your trip. So, you will need a place to store your boots until you get to the trailhead. It's a good idea to store your boots in the cab of the vehicle. If at all possible, *don't* store them in the trunk or any place where they will be exposed to outside temperatures. It's very difficult to keep your feet cozy if you let your boots get very cold before you put them on.

Once on the trail, remember that you'll have a hard time keeping your feet warm if you squander heat by leaving your head uncovered when you're inactive, or if you wear insufficient insulation on your legs, a mistake many people make.

Paul Svetlik

Clothing

The body faces a challenge every day—maintaining a constant internal temperature. A day of snowshoeing puts monumental demands on this heating system. As you snowshoe, your internal furnace generates a great deal of heat. Even in cold temperatures, much of it needs to be ventilated and dissipated. However, when you slow down or stop, you must conserve some of this heat with insulation. Your clothing system plays a major role in regulating your body temperature during a day of snowshoeing.

How the Body Loses Heat

Our biological heating system has five primary ways of venting heat. When you need to shed heat, these mechanisms are your allies. When you must conserve it, they're your adversaries.

- Conduction: Because heat flows from warm surfaces to cold surfaces, you lose heat through conduction when your body touches colder objects. Thus, if you sit on the cold ground in the winter, some body heat will flow to the ground. Water is an excellent conductor, which is why you must avoid getting your clothing wet. In fact, water's heat-draining capability is a large consideration in the design of modern fabrics for outside wear.

- Convection: You lose heat by convection each time the wind blows against your body. The body warms the air close to the skin. In a calm environment, the warm air dissipates slowly. But when wind removes that warm air, your internal furnace must work harder to replace it.

- Radiation: You've probably heard the maxim, "If your feet are cold, put your hat on." It's good advice. The body constantly emits heat, and an uncovered head can radiate so much heat that little is left to be transported to the feet.

- Evaporation: The body uses heat to change moisture into water vapor. This process—evaporation—dissipates a lot of heat. In fact, in summer, evaporating perspiration off the skin is an essential cooling mechanism. In the winter, however, this process can be deadly, not only because it drains energy, but also because sweating can soak your clothing, increasing conductive heat loss.

- Respiration: Every time you inhale, your body heats and humidifies the incoming air so it doesn't damage the lungs. When you exhale, you lose the warmed air. With the next breath, the cycle starts again. Actually, the heat loss from respiration results from a combination of evaporation and convection. It's such a significant source of heat loss, however, that I'm listing it here as a separate mechanism.

Summing Up the Heat-Loss Mechanisms

Take a look at our poorly equipped snowshoer (page 74). She is traveling without any extra gear. She's radiating lots of her body's heat from her uncovered head, while the wind's convection is sweeping away still more. She is losing, by conduction, some heat to the tree she's leaning against. As she breathes, her body uses up heat to warm and humidify the cold air. She is losing still more heat via evaporation from her skin, especially if she has worked up a sweat before stopping. To compound her problems, she's about to get wet from melting snow. Unless she's close to the trailhead, she's in big trouble. She's a candidate for hypothermia (see page 117), a condition that kills many unwary outdoor enthusiasts.

The Three-Part Layering System

To work well during a snowshoeing trip, a clothing system must allow you to dissipate or conserve heat as needed. Outdoor enthusi-

A prime candidate for hypothermia.

asts long ago learned to regulate heat by using a three-part clothing system—an inner, a middle, and an outer layer. Middle and outer layers are added and removed as necessary. Wool was popular with earlier generations because it maintains much of its insulating ability when wet. Recently, scientists have developed a new generation of fabrics that do not absorb moisture and have excellent insulating properties.

Whether your layering system is traditional or modern, it should:

Allow you to shed clothing when you're active and add insulating clothing when you rest

Protect you from the convective effects of the wind

Keep you from getting wet from rain or snow

The Modern Layering System

Modern layering handles the three basic needs. It also adds a new dimension, the ability to move moisture away from your body. Perspiration moves through modern clothing layers to the outside air instead of getting trapped in the clothing. This "moisture management" sets modern clothing apart from traditional clothing.

The Inner Layer

The inner layer, the layer next to the skin, should be your thermal underwear. This is where moisture management begins. Thermals not only keep you warm, but they also wick moisture off your skin, passing it through to the next layer. Modern thermals are made of synthetic fabrics. The earliest fabric, polypropylene, tended to retain odors, even after being laundered.

This is no longer a problem. Some of the more recently developed thermal layers contain an anti-microbial finish to retard odors.

The Middle Layer

The middle, or insulating, layer is the shirt and pants you wear all day, plus the vests, sweaters, and jackets you carry for when the temperature or your activity level drops.

From left, the inner, middle, and outer layers.

Synthetic middle layers are breathable and are made of hydrophobic—literally, "water-fearing" (water-repelling)—fleece. They are good at trapping air warmed by the body, and because they are nonabsorbent, they allow perspiration vapor to pass through. Some fleeces even have a water-resistant finish, enabling them to provide protection during a light snow. Fleece clothing comes in different weights, so snowshoers can select a garment suitable for the conditions they expect to encounter.

Most fleece clothing does not have much wind-stopping ability. This is not always a problem; you may welcome a gentle, cooling breeze, especially when going uphill. Fleece clothing with a wind barrier is available, however; but it does cost more.

Other Options

Sometimes, particularly in the spring, the temperature is not all that cold, and thermals, along with a middle layer, can be much more insulation than you really need. Fortunately, there are options. BiPolar technology is now available, resulting in fabrics that are different on the inside and the outside. The inside layer whisks away the moisture, while the outside of the fabric is hydrophobic and will not absorb water. This technology makes it possible to get by with just a single layer that does the work of two on those days when you don't need the amount of insulation provided by two layers.

The Outer Layer

The outer shell jacket and pants protect against rain, snow, and wind. These garments should allow perspiration vapor to continue its transit through your clothing to the outside air. In short, they should be waterproof and breathable.

Thirty years ago, jackets or pants that were both waterproof and breathable were unheard of. In 1976, W. L. Gore and Associates introduced the Gore-Tex membrane that allows perspiration vapor to escape but prevents rain or snow from penetrating.

Gore-Tex membranes have some 9 billion microscopic pores per square inch. The pores are large enough to allow perspiration to escape but too small to permit rain or wet snow to penetrate. The Gore-Tex membrane is hidden, laminated to the inside of the outer shell fabric and covered by an inner liner.

Manufacturers have introduced several other waterproof/breathable technologies since the introduction of the Gore-Tex membrane. The microporous coating is one of them. These coatings, which also have billions of

Dennis Welsh

Wear all three layers before heading out—it's important not to lose body heat.

microscopic pores, are applied to the inside of the outer shell fabric. Many manufacturers market their own brands of waterproof/breathable shell clothing that use this technology.

Some shells use a SympaTex membrane, a nonporous layer laminated to a suitable outer fabric. Its waterproof and breathable characteristics are achieved through a combination of chemical and physical principles. You will also find "smart" fabrics, such as Marmot's MemBrain, which has a micro-thin laminate of temperature-sensitive molecule strands that change shape to allow more breathability during high activity.

While modern outer shells are wonderful, don't expect miracles. There's a limit to how much perspiration vapor they can dissipate. If you're working hard climbing and it starts snowing or raining, you've got to put on an outer shell. However, you're adding a layer when you'd normally shed one to cool off. Situations like this can overload the breathability of the outer shell.

Just how waterproof are these shells? It all comes down to pounds per square inch of water-entry pressure the garment can withstand. As a frame of reference, W. L. Gore and Associates notes in its literature that a 165-pound person exerts about 3 pounds per square inch of pressure on a fabric when seated and about 16 pounds per square inch when kneeling. Its Gore-Tex fabric can withstand 65 pounds per square inch of the pressure exerted by pelting rain—water-entry pressure. Water-resistant or water-repellent garments, on the other hand, can repel less than 1 pound per square inch of water-entry pressure. Manufacturers can generally tell you how much water-entry pressure their clothing can withstand.

In some parts of North America, such as higher elevations in the Rockies, winter temperatures are usually very low and the snow does not contain much moisture. In such circumstances a snowshoer can use a microfiber shell jacket and shell pants that are highly water-resistant but not truly waterproof. A *microfiber* fabric, made of very fine fibers woven very tightly, blocks wind and repels water but still permits perspiration vapors to escape. Since microfiber shells are more breathable than most waterproof/breathable fabrics, they are useful if you will be expending lots of energy in an environment that does not produce rain or wet snow.

Once you have chosen the type of outer shell you will purchase, make sure you buy one that is large enough to wear over your middle layers.

The Traditional Layering System

Our grandparents successfully used a three-part layering system that depended on wool and down for the first two layers, and separate windproof and waterproof shells for the outer layer. Many people still use this system, or portions of it, to stay comfortable.

In the traditional layering system, the inner layer is thermal underwear made of wool or wool blends. If it becomes damp from perspiration, it still keeps you warm. The middle layer consists of wool shirts and pants, as well as a vest or jacket. The latter are usually made with goose or duck down. Down jackets are wonderful. Their warmth-to-weight ratio is excellent. However, down has two major drawbacks; when wet, down clumps together, ruining its insulating ability, and if the jacket tears, the down blows away. Both situations are bad news if you're far from the trailhead.

Many synthetic fibers have been used to

replace down. Some of these synthetics are still in use, and more are being developed. None surpasses down in its insulating power, but most do retain some of their insulating ability when wet. But, they don't have the moisture management capability of today's fleece.

The traditional outer layer requires two separate outer shells—a breathable one for wind protection and a non-breathable one for rain protection. Twenty years ago, the traditional wind shell was usually made of a blend of cotton and polyester, a combination that breathes well and provides good wind resistance. However, older rain suits, made of coated nylon or some other waterproof fabric, don't breathe, and it doesn't take long for the wool layers underneath to get soaked from perspiration.

Comparing the Modern and Traditional Systems

Moisture management is the main difference between modern and traditional layering. The modern system has it—the traditional system doesn't. In addition, modern clothing is easily laundered, quick drying, and a joy to wear. It's also expensive. Completely outfitting yourself with all three layers can put a serious dent in your checkbook. You may be able, however, to put together an inexpensive wardrobe just by looking through your closet for some old wool shirts and pants, and maybe even an old down jacket. These woolen and down items will serve you well as long as your snowshoeing ambitions remain modest.

Although no longer the garments of choice among many of us who journey to the hills to rekindle our bond with nature, wool is still preferred by many people in the far north in this country and in Canada, folks for whom snowshoeing and outside activity are necessity, not recreation. In these places, wool has passed the test of time—people live and work outdoors in wool clothing and they have found it to be durable, affordable, and effective. Thus, even though you will have a difficult time finding wool products among the offerings at most popular mountaineering shops, fine wool clothing suitable for strenuous outdoor life is still made and is available. You can find a list of suppliers in Garrett and Alexandra Conover's book, *A Snow Walker's Companion*, listed in Appendix C.

One final point is very important. Avoid cotton clothing in the winter. Cotton clothing can be deadly. It absorbs moisture easily and loses its insulating value when it gets wet.

Hybrid Systems

Many people draw from both new and traditional clothing for their snowshoeing wardrobe. For instance, as old-style garments wear out, many veteran snowshoers replace them piece by piece with more modern counterparts.

A hybrid system, using the woolen clothing and down jackets you already have, is an economical way to get started. Once you become hooked on snowshoeing, you can slowly acquire more modern clothing. Make synthetic thermals your first new acquisition, followed by a waterproof and breathable shell.

Head Gear

Because the body loses a lot of heat through an uncovered head, adequate, layered head gear is essential. A simple wool cap is a good insulating layer, while the hood of a shell jacket can be the outer layer, providing protection against wind and precipitation.

Hats range from simple wool caps to more sophisticated models with Gore-Tex and other modern components. Outdoor shops and catalogs carry hats in many models and degrees of sophistication. Some have visors to shield the face from the sun and falling snow. Others have foldable earflaps. Another option is a balaclava, which can be used as a hat or as a combination hat and face mask.

In very cold weather, masks are critical for protecting the face from frostbite. Both neoprene and fleece models work well, but try on a prospective purchase to make sure it fits well and that you can breath easily through it.

Neck gaiters, which are sleeves of wool, syn- thetic fiber, or fleece that can be pulled over the head to keep the neck warm, are worthy of a place in with your head gear. Wool or fleece headbands are also handy. Occasions arise when you are working hard, such as when climbing—and you want to ventilate and dissipate some heat through your head, but you want to protect your ears at the same time; headbands work nicely in such situations.

Mittens and Gloves

Mittens are warmer than gloves because they present less surface area to the cold and allow the fingers to keep each other warm. Layering

Proper headgear, including face covers for very cold weather, is vital.

helps. Putting a Gore-Tex outer shell over a pair of fleece or heavy wool mittens adds protection from wind and precipitation. Outdoor Research, Inc., makes excellent Gore-Tex shells. Dachstein mittens, made of 100 percent boiled wool, have been popular for many years. Boiling enhances their water and wind resistance.

Sometimes it's necessary to remove mittens to perform a task that requires using your fingers. To temporarily protect your hands from the cold while allowing dexterity, bring along thin wool or synthetic gloves, or gloves with half-fingers that cover all of the hand except the fingertips.

Because hand protection is so important, pack a spare pair of mittens (or use a spare pair of heavy socks) large enough to fit the biggest member of your group.

An Outdoor Wardrobe on a Budget

To find clothing on a limited budget, try the local thrift store. You may be amazed by what you find, maybe even a Gore-Tex jacket or pants. Shell jackets and pants with a Gore-Tex membrane will have a Gore-Tex label inside, so they are easy to identify. They may not be as good as the latest models in the stores, but they will serve beginners well.

If you buy a used Gore-Tex jacket, test it at home to see how waterproof it is. Put the jacket over some paper towels on the floor and pour some water on it. Let the water remain for a few minutes. The seams at the shoulders and in the hood are critical because they bear the brunt of heavy rain or snow, so make sure they are saturated. Then, soak up the surface water and lift up the jacket. If the paper towels under the jacket remain dry, the

jacket is probably reasonably waterproof. If you find some leaks, buy a bottle of seam sealer or tape designed to seal seams. In addition, after laundering the jacket, spray it with a water-repellent finish.

The economy-minded snowshoer will also search thrift shops for fleece jackets, wool pants and shirts, down and synthetic jackets and vests, windbreakers, coated nylon rain suits, hats, mittens, neck gaiters, wool socks, and even winter boots. The condition of available items may not be perfect, but good used garments are more than adequate for easy recreational trips.

Clothing for Children

Fleece clothing for children abounds at your local outdoor shop. You can also find waterproof/breathable shell clothing for them there. However, because children are growing, it might not be wise to outfit them with the most expensive clothing. Also, you will probably be doing easy recreational trips with your children, so you might be able to get by with clothing you already have. If you can't find anything in the closet, the local thrift shops again are an excellent place to begin. Remember to stay away from cotton. Pay particular attention to the socks; make sure they provide insulation. And, make sure the boots your child wears are not too tight, or your little snowshoer will soon have cold feet and want to go home.

If you do plan to purchase some new items, begin with new liner socks and thermal underwear designed to move moisture away from the body. These items will add to your child's overall comfort. You will find that contemporary high-tech clothing has some nice features, such as thumb holes to keep the sleeves from riding up. Regardless of whether you plan to use clothes you already have or new ones, follow the principles of layering, and be prepared to help children with their layers throughout the day. If it's cold at the trailhead, start them off with all their layers on, but check them periodically to see if it's time to shed a layer or two.

Packs

Any snowshoer who heads into the mountains and forests must carry a pack with food, water, and extra gear. Always be prepared; emergencies can occur on even the most laid-back trips.

The Fundamentals of Pack Selection

A good pack should be comfortable, durable, and able to hold needed gear. Padded shoulder straps, a waist belt, a padded back, and an internal frame can increase comfort. To be most useful, a pack must have carrying capacity equal to your gear load and offer easy access to that gear.

Basic Designs

Packs come in three basic designs:

- Top-loading rucksacks have one large compartment with a drawstring closure at the top and a flap that cinches down with quick-release buckles. This design eliminates potential problems with large zippers—such as breaking, leaking, or getting stuck. Some models also have small side pockets or a front pocket. Their carrying capacity can be extended by layering extra clothing under the top flap, as long as the weather is good. A drawback of rucksacks is that you must remove items at the top to reach those at the bottom.

A good pack is essential gear for all but the shortest of trips: left, a panel-loading pack, right, a lumbar pack.

- Panel-loading packs have a zipper that runs in an arc across the front of the pack. The unzipped front flap folds down, exposing all the gear for easy access. Some models have zippered upper and lower compartments. While zippers can break, top-quality packs have heavy-duty zippers that provide years of service.

- Lumbar packs are worn around the waist. While earlier versions were not large enough for winter gear, some of today's lumbar packs have enough capacity to carry what you need on a snowshoeing day trip.

Cliff Leight

Capacity

Winter gear takes up a lot of space. Get a pack that easily handles all your gear without overstuffing. Manufacturers' hang-tags will usually tell the cubic inches of storage space. A daytime recreational outing in winter weather requires at least 1,600 to 2,000 cubic inches of storage. Overnight trips require at least 3,500 cubic inches of storage, and more is better. External pockets can be added to some packs.

Shoulder and Waist Straps

Padded shoulder straps are standard on first-rate top- or panel-loading packs. Many will also have sternum straps that cinch together across your chest, keeping the shoulder straps from slipping.

The pack should also have a waist strap for added stability. On smaller packs of the type suitable for easy recreational trips, a nylon strap with a quick-release buckle is all you'll need. Packs with larger capacities usually have a padded waist belt, which helps to transfer weight to the hips and makes a heavier load *much* more comfortable.

Padded Back

All but the smallest backpacks have backs that are padded, usually with a dense foam. Padding helps shape the pack and prevents hard things—like a water bottle or thermos—from poking you in the back.

Larger and more upscale packs may have an internal frame, which helps to distribute the load more evenly; these are good for longer trips that require more than just the basic gear.

Weight

Many suitable packs with padded shoulder straps, a padded back, and a waist belt weigh less than 2 pounds. The more upscale packs with internal frames weigh a bit more.

Choosing Your Pack

Check out all three designs. Remember that the most important quality of a pack is comfort, which you'll only be able to judge by trying it on, loaded with the weight you expect to carry. The sales staff at a good outdoor shop should be willing to fill the pack for you. Since smaller, less expensive packs come in only one size, without many options for customizing the fit, make sure the one you want fits your build.

Dennis Welsh

What to Put in Your Pack

The clothing you add and shed throughout the day goes in your pack. The pack also holds lots of liquid, lunch, snacks, and the safety essentials.

Water

Carry at least one quart of water for an easy recreational outing, and more for longer trips. As previously noted, cold air is very dry and removes much of the body's moisture. Stop periodically to drink, even if you're not thirsty; the sensation of thirst lags behind your actual need for water.

Many water bottle varieties are available, including several high-quality models made by Nalgene Trail Products. A number of manufacturers make insulated covers that will keep the bottle's contents from freezing and will keep a hot beverage reasonably warm. The ones made from closed-cell foam work best. You can also make your own out of some closed-cell foam and duct tape. Two different sizes are available commercially; one fits Nalgene's half-liter bottles and the other fits liter bottles. Nalgene's loop-top bottle plus an insulating cover make an excellent combination. Herb tea with honey tastes great on a cold day and will stay pleasantly warm inside your insulated water bottle.

Lunch and Snacks

Don't try to diet on snowshoeing days—you will need many more calories than you need on a day in the office. Make sure to eat before you go, bring along lunch and snacks, and pack a thermos of hot soup or tea.

Safety Essentials

Carry and know how to use a map and compass. If you follow well-marked trails below treeline on a nice day, you probably won't need them; but if you're traveling above treeline or will be in any exposed areas, you must know how to use both in order to find your way back to the trailhead. Storms can move in with amazing speed, and wind and blowing snow can quickly cover your tracks.

Either a flashlight or a headlamp should be part of your emergency gear; many prefer a headlamp because it leaves the hands free. You should also always bring matches in a waterproof container and fire starters for building an emergency fire in case you are caught off guard by severe conditions or forced to spend the night out; windproof and stormproof matches can be very handy. Carrying a lighter in addition to matches is a good idea, too; the lighter may need to be warmed by your hands before it will light. Fire starters are inexpensive, lightweight, and readily available in sporting goods shops.

For a personal emergency shelter, you can use three large plastic bags, which can also serve as emergency rain or wind protection. Your personal shelter can also be a lightweight emergency blanket made of space-age material. The single-use variety weighs about 4 ounces and costs around $3. Also available is an emergency bag made of similar space-age material that weighs only a few ounces and costs around $10. An even better choice for emergency shelter is a slightly heavier emergency blanket (about 12 ounces) with a higher tensile strength and grommets in

The Recreational Snowshoer's Safety Essentials

The unexpected can always happen. To handle emergencies on the trail, always carry the "safety essentials" in your pack:

Map

Compass

Flashlight or headlamp with a spare bulb and extra batteries

Matches (in a waterproof container) and several fire starters

Emergency shelter

Extra food and water

Extra clothing

Knife

Sun protection (glasses and cream)

First-aid kit

Cup

Wire pocket saw

Whistle

Safety essentials.

the corners. MPI Outdoor Safety Products markets one called an All Weather Blanket, and it is available in many stores that carry outdoor gear. This heavy-duty blanket is 5 feet by 7 feet and is red on one side and silver on the other. It costs about $12. It can easily be turned into an emergency shelter below timberline using the instructions on page 103 and is, in fact, a multi-use item that can be used as a windbreaker or as a signaling device for air rescue. The red side should be used for signaling on snow.

Carry extra food and water—beyond what you plan to consume during your outing. Emergency food is your reserve energy supply if your return home is delayed. Include complex carbohydrates and items with high caloric value, such as meal replacement bars. You'll find lots of tasty food bars at your local outdoor shop. Although not specifically on the list of essentials, it is a good idea to carry a bottle of water purification tablets or iodine crystals; water in the wild is no longer safe to drink unless it has been boiled, filtered, or treated. You could also carry a filter, but these weigh more than the tablets or crystals and can freeze.

Pack an extra layer of clothing—beyond what you plan to put on and take off during your trip. A heavy wool shirt, a fleece sweater, or a fleece or down vest can serve the purpose. If an emergency causes a delay in your return or even an unexpected night spent out in the elements, you are likely to experience a chilling temperature drop. That extra insulating layer will keep you warm. Also include an extra hat, mittens, and socks with your extra clothing.

A knife, also a safety essential, can be useful on any trip. It can cut bandages in first aid situations and serve countless other purposes. When you're outdoors, far from the conve-

niences of hardware stores and repair shops, all sorts of unexpected needs tend to crop up, and a knife will often be just the thing to attend to those needs. Not to mention that block of cheese that needs slicing. Swiss Army knives are excellent; many models have a small scissors and tweezers.

Sun protection is essential on all trips. Protect your eyes and skin from the sun with sunglasses and sunscreen. Put sunscreen on before you start the trip, and then add more during the day as directed by the manufacturer. Use Sun Protection Factor 15 or higher and be sure to cover all exposed parts of the body. Don't forget to use a protective balm on your lips. Spring snowshoeing trips present additional sun hazards, because in the warmer temperatures you'll probably be peeling off layers of clothing, sometimes right down to your skin. If you do, make sure you apply sunscreen to the newly exposed areas.

Your sunglasses are necessary on most trips. Because snow reflects light, you should look for sunglasses that absorb at least 80 percent of the visible light and more than 90 percent of ultraviolet radiation. For extreme situations, you will find glacier glasses that absorb more than 90 percent of visible light. For blowing snow, you will need goggles, although the design of some contemporary sunglasses, with their wrap-around features, are adequate for all but the most severe conditions.

For easy to moderate trips, a first aid kit should include adhesive bandages, antiseptic towelettes, antiseptic cream, moleskin for blisters, sterile gauze wrap, sterile pads, adhesive tape, aspirin or acetaminophen, antacid tablets, an anti-diarrhea medication, an Ace bandage, and tweezers. You might want to carry a small first aid manual in case you have forgotten some of the finer points of emergency care. The Mountaineers publishes one that is 35 pages long, weighs about 1 ounce, and is packed with information. It costs less than $3. You can find a number of other pocket-size manuals in outdoor shops.

In a group situation, one first aid kit should be sufficient. However, you should still carry a mini-first aid kit of your own, with moleskin for blisters, antiseptic towelettes, aspirin or acetaminophen, and adhesive bandages, plus any medications that you need. Commercial first aid kits are available from several manufacturers if you don't want to put together your own. You will probably find a large selection at your local outdoor shop. Remember to check your first aid kit occasionally to see that none of the contents is beyond expiration date.

Many mountaineers recommend that you carry a thin pad of closed-cell foam to prevent conductive heat loss to the ground. You can use it at lunchtime or in a survival situation. This inexpensive foam is frequently used to make sleeping pads. Some outdoor shops sell pieces just large enough to sit on, or you can

buy a whole pad and cut off what you need.

A small repair kit should include duct tape, parachute cord, and several large safety pins. The tape can be used for repairing clothing and damaged equipment. The parachute cord—at least 100 feet of it—has many uses. With it, you can lash items to your pack, make emergency repairs to equipment, and construct an emergency shelter out of your all-weather blanket.

You should carry an inexpensive wire pocket saw. This, too, weighs only a few ounces and can be used to cut wood for an emergency fire.

It is a good idea to carry a metal cup that can be used for melting snow and heating water over an emergency fire. Keep aluminum foil with the cup to serve as a cover.

Another inexpensive item to include is a whistle, which can serve as a signaling device in an emergency. It's a good idea to give a whistle to any children in your party, with instructions to use it if they accidentally find themselves separated from the group.

Carrying extra toe warmers and pocket

Emergency Snowshoes

The weather forecast for your backcountry trip had been promising, and you planned accordingly. But Mother Nature pulled a surprise and dumped very heavy snow on the five miles between you and your car. It's possible to make "emergency snowshoes" if you're below timberline.

If you're not walking too far, evergreen branches lashed to your feet with parachute cord are a possibility. If you don't have any cord, use branches to construct a binding. Or use green saplings to make a bearpaw

snowshoe. Bend the branch and lash the ends together. Weave additional evergreen branches into the frame to form a deck.

If you're intrigued about the possibilities, you'll find some additional information in *Camping and Wilderness Survival* by Paul Tawrell, *A Snow Walker's Companion: Winter Trail Skills from the Far North* by Garrett and Alexandra Conover, and *The Snowshoe Book,* Second Edition, by William Osgood and Leslie Hurley (see Appendix C for more information).

warmers is a good idea. They provide an instant source of heat to use during any emergency. You will also find larger warmers that are inexpensive, generate about 135 degrees Fahrenheit for 12 hours, and weigh only a few ounces.

When Nature Calls

Toilet tissue is another important, though certainly not lifesaving, item to bring along in your pack. At your outdoor shop you will find small rolls designed specifically for the backpacker. Because of the large number of people who now head to the mountains and forests, where there generally are no privies, handling nature's call has become a great concern to environmentalists. You should always make your temporary latrine at least 200 feet from the nearest stream or lake. An entire book, with the very catchy title *How to shit in the woods*, has been written on this subject, and it sheds light on the seriousness of this concern. You will find it listed in Appendix C.

Paul Svetlik

Packing Your Gear

We all differ in how organized we normally are. When packing outdoor gear, however, organization is essential:

- As you gather gear before a trip, put related items, such as first aid kit components, into separate pouches or plastic boxes.

- Put extra clothing in inexpensive stuff sacks; doing so will keep your pack organized and your clothing dry. If you don't have stuff sacks, use plastic sacks.

- Extra food should be kept in a separate sack or container, as should emergency gear such as your fire starter, flashlight, and personal shelter.

- Stow emergency gear toward the bottom of the pack; odds are you won't need it, but you'll always know where it is. Put the food and water you plan to consume during the trip and your clothing that you plan to use for the day near the top.

- Keep water very handy since it's important to drink regularly.

Part Four

Backcountry Treks

Doug Berry, Outside Images

and Racing

Chapter Six

Backcountry Snowshoeing

Cliff Leight

As you start hiking farther from the trailhead, venturing off established trails to see more remote areas, traveling above treeline, or climbing peaks, you are leaving the recreational realm and entering the world of backcountry snowshoeing. You'll know when you've made the passage. And you'll know that you need more gear, more stamina, and more training. The backcountry is beautiful, but it can also be unforgiving, even deadly, especially in the winter. You can't make many mistakes in the backcountry and live to tell about them.

Equipment is not the only issue when it comes to backcountry snowshoeing. Before you get started you need to fine-tune your navigational skills, learn wilderness survival skills, and be physically prepared for the challenges. Even the best equipment cannot compensate for lack of knowledge or physical fitness.

The Traditional Backcountry Snowshoe

Traditional laced, wood-frame snowshoes were designed for rugged use. They were, indeed, the original backcountry snowshoes. In fact, there truly was nothing *but* backcountry for the thousands of years during which traditional wood-frame snowshoes were perfected. But they don't perform very well in steep terrain, and today the backcountry has increasingly come to mean the mountains. For those fortunate enough to live in areas where snowshoeing is a way of life and not a recreational pursuit, and in those areas where the backcountry has deep powder and open terrain without steep slopes, the traditional wood-frame snowshoe is suitable, and it does a superior job of providing flotation in deep snow. It is important, however, to use it only in the terrain for which it was designed.

If you would like a wood-frame snowshoe with a bit more technology applied to it, you should look at the Tubbs model with backcountry bindings and crampons attached. You should also look at the Freetrail and Winter Hiker lines developed by Faber and Company.

The Aluminum-Frame Backcountry Snowshoe

If you're heading into the mountains with the intention of doing some serious uphill trekking, you should use an aluminum-frame backcountry snowshoe or a general-purpose snowshoe that the manufacturer recommends for such use.

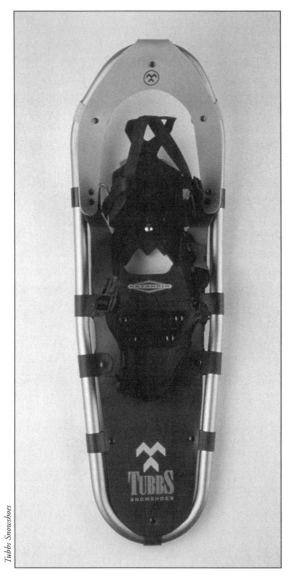

A Tubbs backcountry model.

Tubbs Snowshoes

The basic components of the aluminum-frame snowshoes intended for backcountry use are discussed in "Snowshoe Design" (see pages 20–29). Snowshoe designers craft these components—the frame, deck, pivot system, bindings, and traction device—into snowshoes that handle difficult and steep terrain with ease. What differentiates these snowshoes from the recreational variety is the extremely rugged nature of these same components. General-purpose snowshoes will usually also have these same heavy-duty components. You should never head into the backcountry on entry-level snowshoes or snowshoes designed specifically for recreational use or running. They simply do not have the necessary rugged hardware.

When you begin shopping for your snowshoes, it is important to know the terms various manufacturers use to distinguish their backcountry series. Some do call them "backcountry" snowshoes; but others call them their "backpacking" series, their "hiking" series, or their "altitude" series. You can easily tell the difference between recreational and backcountry models from the same manufacturer simply by looking at them. The backcountry ones have bigger traction devices and sturdier bindings, and they generally weigh more and cost more. However, since many outdoor shops do not carry all models from a given manufacturer, you might not be able to make the comparison visually. Check with the salesperson to make sure the pair you are considering is a backcountry model. If still in doubt, ask to see the manufacturer's brochure, or call the manufacturer and get one. The backcountry models will be clearly identified in the brochure.

Consistent with the trend toward increased specialization, some manufacturers are now

Dennis Welsh

further subdividing their backcountry offerings and adding an even more specialized model, sometimes called a "mountaineering," a "summit," or an "expedition" snowshoe. These top-of-the-line snowshoes are intended for use in extreme conditions. Their ratchet-type, step-in bindings provide the utmost in lateral control. It is on some of these highly specialized snowshoes that you will find bindings that work only with specific types of boots.

The Frame

Backcountry snowshoes have heavy-duty frames that can withstand the abuse of demanding terrain. Both symmetrical and asymmetrical frames are sold, but most manufacturers favor symmetrical designs, perhaps because they provide a bit more flotation—an especially important consideration for backcountry snowshoers, because off-trail terrain is frequently covered with deep snow. So, you have to weigh carefully the benefits of the increased flotation you get with a larger snowshoe against the better maneuverability you get with a smaller one.

The Pivot System

Backcountry snowshoes come with rotating-pivot systems, fixed-pivot systems, and dual systems.

Rotating-Pivot Systems

The backcountry, with its steep terrain and deep snow, is the domain of the rotating-pivot system. The main issues are discussed in "Snowshoe Design" (see pages 23–25). Because the tail of the snowshoe with a rotating-pivot system drags on the ground, snow tends to slide off the deck when the toe of

the snowshoe is raised for the next step. As a result, you save energy because you never have to lift a snowshoe deck loaded with snow. Rotating-pivot systems also provide an energy-efficient way of climbing. Each snowshoer has to decide, however, whether the enhanced climbing ability is worth the decreased maneuverability of this design. Only you can make that determination based on a knowledge of the terrain you expect to cover. As already noted, Tubbs uses this type of pivot system on all its backcountry and expedition models. Sherpa uses it, too, but has modified it to provide "dual rotation," which allows its backcountry snowshoes to perform with fixed-pivot characteristics on packed trails. Yuba also uses a rotating-pivot system on its snowshoes but it limits deck rotation to about 60 degrees.

Fixed-Pivot Systems

Redfeather, Atlas, Northern Lites, Good Thunder, and several other manufacturers now offer backcountry and expedition-quality snowshoes with this highly maneuverable pivot system. Although fixed-pivot snowshoes may not climb the extremely steep slopes with the same energy efficiency as rotating-pivot snowshoes (see pages 25–27), they do have the definite advantage of being more maneuverable in wooded areas where the snowshoer frequently must step over downed timber. As far as snow-shedding ability goes, this design does not do as well as the rotating-pivot system. Nevertheless, some tail dragging and snow shedding does occur with fixed-pivot systems, particularly with the larger models that have longer decks stretching out behind the foot. So don't dismiss fixed-pivot designs when considering backcountry snowshoes. In fact, in 1994, *Backpacker* magazine gave its highest overall rating to an Atlas back-country snowshoe using a patented adaptation of the fixed-pivot design Atlas calls its Spring Loaded Binding.

Summing It Up: Pivot Systems on Backcountry Snowshoes

Each system has its advantages. In addition, the pivot system, even though it is an important component, is still only one part of the snowshoe; you can only judge the overall performance of a backcountry snowshoe by looking at the interaction of all its components. Each snowshoe model is different, and it must work with your unique stride and your personal snowshoeing ambitions. Give equal consideration to the frame shape, bindings, traction devices, and overall design of the snowshoe when you make your selection.

The Bindings

The bindings on backcountry snowshoes provide superior lateral control, which is essential when you are climbing, descending, and traversing—all activities typical of back-country snowshoeing. Designs using the rotating-pivot system, because of the stiffness of the pivot rod, offer excellent lateral control.

The rubber-like strap used on fixed-pivot designs, however, does not provide this same stiffness; therefore, designers working with fixed-pivot systems frequently include a molded footbed or some other device to enhance the lateral stability of their back-country snowshoes.

You'll find many types of bindings available on backcountry snowshoes. Most allow you to use any type of winter boot or hiking boot. This characteristic is also true of general-purpose snowshoes. Among the upscale backcountry models—those expedition, summit, or mountaineering snowshoes—you will see bindings that may require specific types of boots.

Traction Devices

The hefty traction devices on many back-country snowshoes look like they belong in the Grand Inquisitor's arsenal. If someone stepped on you with one, you'd be on your way to the hospital. Traction devices on back-country snowshoes have a more aggressive design than those found on recreational snowshoes, and they range in length from 1 to 1½ inches or more. They are designed to provide gripping power on difficult terrain.

Transitioning between Sports

For some folks, snowshoes provide a way to travel into an area to snowboard, ski, or ice climb. The snowshoeing industry has taken careful note of the impact these other sports have had on the current boom in snowshoeing. In response, some manufacturers offer special bindings and packages that mount on the snowshoes and allow the snowshoer to use boots designed for the related sport. No lugging along a second pair of boots, no sinking or falling into powder as you try to switch footwear, no snow-covered socks if you lose your balance. Tubbs offers its Nordic Base Plate package for cross-country skiers and its Snowboard Base Plate for snowboarders. Redfeather offers an optional binding to use with snowboarding boots.

How do you find out about transitioning devices and special bindings and equipment? It's difficult to give general advice because of the many changes in bindings and related products that seem to take place each year. Begin by looking at the bindings and snowshoes in local shops to see if anything meets your needs. If you need something more specialized, ask the salespeople at the shop if optional binding packages are available. If they don't know, check with several manufacturers about their products and tell them of your specific needs. The manufacturers can give you expert advice on additional products or specific models of their snowshoes that may work for you.

Injection-Molded Backcountry Snowshoes

These snowshoes, which have been in use in Europe for many years, are making their way into the marketplace in this country. Many of the models and bindings available from TSL and Boldas, two French companies, have very sophisticated bindings and have been

designed for use on difficult terrain. The market in this country is still very much dominated by the aluminum-frame backcountry snowshoe, but these injection-molded ones do represent a new option.

Clothing

Backcountry snowshoers encounter more severe temperature and weather conditions and need more layers of clothing than are required for easy trips on gentle terrain. Several layers of fleece will do the job. Down has long been used in clothing designed for

extremely cold weather but lost its dominant position because it becomes useless if it gets wet. Many of the problems associated with down, however, have been minimized with the introduction of DryLoft fabric by W. L. Gore and Associates.

DryLoft Fabric and Down Insulation

DryLoft fabric was designed for use with down clothing and sleeping bags. In the past, down lost its loft—and thus its insulating qualities—when saturated with water either from precipitation from the outside or perspiration from the inside. DryLoft was designed to minimize the moisture problem associated with down.

DryLoft fabric is extremely breathable, water-resistant, and windproof. Its enhanced breathability allows perspiration vapor to move quickly through the fabric before it can saturate the down. This helps to eliminate a large part of the moisture problem. It is not waterproof, however. A waterproof/breathable shell must be used over it in wet snow or rain. Down clothing and sleeping bags designed for mountaineering trips are made with DryLoft.

Footgear

Felt-lined pack boots, double-leather boots, and double-plastic boots have been available for backcountry use for many years. Unfortunately, these usually weigh 4 pounds or more per pair.

In 1997, Technica, in consultation with Tubbs Snowshoe Company, developed a boot specifically for snowshoeing. This boot, The Snow Paw, weighs less than 3 pounds. It has a Pressure Distribution Plate (PDP) that sits on top of the tongue and distributes over a large area the pressure exerted by the binding's laces or instep strap. The instep strap or other closure that rests on this plate can therefore be tightened to enhance heel retention in the binding without causing pain. The boot has insulation in the toe area, a waterproof/breathable liner, and an aggressive lug sole.

Pay careful attention to the weight of the boots you're considering and select the lightest boots that will serve your needs. But avoid three-season hiking boots; they won't be warm enough in the backcountry. The warmth of winter boots can be enhanced with modern socks and toe warmers, and several manufacturers now offer insulated bindings with their backcountry snowshoes.

Gaiters are a necessary part of backcountry equipment. Beefed-up versions, the "super gaiters," are designed especially for extremely cold weather. Some models have insulation. You will also find overboots that can be used in extreme conditions. So there's no reason to suffer with cold feet, even in very cold temperatures.

Mukluks are an option for the backcountry traveler, but they are not suitable for terrain that might require crampons or walking without snowshoes. Also, you should not use them if you will be carrying a heavy pack or doing a lot of climbing, because they do not provide the ankle support found on mountaineering boots. However, mukluks are very warm and are a good choice for expeditions in which the gear is transported on sleds.

Backcountry Dangers

Traveling in the mountains and forests in the winter always presents an element of danger. The danger increases as you go deeper into the wilderness or climb peaks. Whiteouts are common, wind and blowing snow are routine, and avalanches are a reality in many parts of the country.

The dangers of sunburn and snowblindness increase at higher elevations. If you aren't prepared, you could seriously damage your eyes or skin, or at least experience considerable pain. Make sure your sunglasses have side shields and can absorb at least 80 percent of the visible light, and more than 90 percent of the ultraviolet rays. Carry a pair of goggles in case you encounter blowing snow. Lens color makes a big difference in how you see. Gray and green lenses give the truest colors, while yellow lenses give the best visibility in overcast conditions. If you will be at high altitudes on snowfields, you should have a pair of glacier glasses that can absorb more than 90 percent of the visible light. In an emergency, if you find yourself or a member of your group without eye protection, you can improvise by cutting small slits in an eye cover made from cloth or a bandanna.

Also be aware that any medical problem becomes more serious in the backcountry because you are far from help. Upgrading your first aid skills increases your margin of safety in emergencies.

What to Bring Along

You'll need to bring along everything you needed on an easy trip (see pages 86–87), plus more, so a large, comfortable pack is necessary—something with a least 2,000 cubic inches of storage room, and preferably more. You might want to consider a pack with an internal frame. These packs distribute the weight very well and stay close to the back, enabling the user to maintain good balance even when the pack is heavy.

Safety Essentials for the Backcountry

Map
Compass
Flashlight or headlamp with a spare bulb
    and extra batteries
Knife
Matches (in a waterproof container) and
    several fire starters
Emergency shelter (heavy-duty all-weather
    blanket with grommets and at least 100
    feet of parachute cord)
Closed-cell foam pad
First aid kit
Extra food and water
Extra clothing
Shovel (for shelter building and avalanche
    safety)
Sun protection
Toe and pocket warmers
Avalanche gear (if you're in avalanche
    country): probe poles, avalanche trans-
    ceiver, shovel (see above)
Pocket saw
Repair kit
Metal cup and aluminum foil
Whistle

Handling Emergencies

If you have an emergency that forces you to spend an unexpected night in the backcountry, you will need to use your safety essentials and related gear to survive the cold nighttime temperatures. If you are below timberline, you can build an emergency shelter using your all-weather blanket and parachute cord. The advantages of this type of shelter are that it can be set up quickly and that it allows you to build a warming fire in front of it. Begin by selecting a place that is sheltered from strong winds. Make sure the place you select is not in the runout zone of an avalanche or near any sick or dead trees that might blow down. Then tie some parachute cord between two trees,

approximately 2 to 2½ feet above the ground. Lay about 4 inches of the blanket over this cord, and then place the back wall of the shelter at a 45 degree angle to the ground, leaving enough blanket to lie on. The 4 inches that overhang the parachute cord can be tied either to a tree or to the main cord. Use the silver side of the blanket for the interior of the shelter.

The next thing you'll need to do is build an emergency fire outside your shelter. Look for dry wood and collect enough to keep the fire going the entire night. Bark from the underside of downed trees makes good kindling. Even wet wood will burn if it is dried by your fire. Build a fire base on the snow using large,

You can craft an emergency shelter from an all-weather blanket and parachute cord.

4-inch diameter or larger wood pieces that you cut with your wire pocket saw. Put the fire starter on the base and surround it with kindling. Then add small sticks over this in teepee style. Light the fire starter and blow lightly to help ignite the kindling. Add progressively larger pieces of wood. Sit or lie inside the shelter on your closed-cell foam pad, which will offer some welcome insulation between you and the snow. If you do not have enough insulation under you, use pine boughs. Eat the emergency food supply you brought, and make sure you drink water. Use your metal cup to melt snow over the fire so that you have enough to drink. For additional protection, you can build a wall of snow around your camp.

You can also make a snow shelter. Building sophisticated snow caves, igloos, and snow trenches takes skill which is best acquired through participation in winter mountaineering classes. Nevertheless, it is possible to build a crude snow trench that will provide shelter. Use your shovel to dig a pit about 8 feet long and 3 feet wide. If you don't have a shovel, use one of your snowshoes. Create a roof over your trench with pine boughs. If you can't find branches, use your snowshoes or poles. Then cover these with snow. You can use your pack to close the entrance. Make sure, however, that you maintain ventilation.

If you browse through books on wilderness survival, you will come upon lots of good information about emergency shelters. Regardless of the terrain or the season, there's always something you can construct to protect yourself from the elements. Never assume there's nothing you can do. And remember, in a survival situation, your brain is your best piece of equipment. Use it.

Planning a Backcountry Trip

Backcountry travel requires more planning than a recreational trip.

Places to Go

The variety of places to go is limited only by your time, ability, and equipment. You can return to familiar trails visited on initial easy outings; you can go farther from the trailhead, perhaps climbing above treeline; or you can explore areas off the trail. Look at books on hiking, cross-country ski trails, and snowshoeing trails, and pick something with more mileage and elevation gain than you experienced on your easier trips.

Organized club trips are a good way to explore new areas. You'll learn how to get there, where to leave the car, and just what the terrain is like. Later, you can return with your friends for further exploration. Going on club trips will also assure that you'll be traveling with people who have comparable technical skills and endurance, a key to safe travel in the backcountry. Most clubs rate trips as easy, moderate, or difficult and give the mileage and elevation gain. They sometimes rate their participants, requiring that prospective trip members have completed certain club schools and seminars before they can go on more challenging trips. This policy weeds out people who

might prevent the group from reaching the trip destination.

Maps and Navigation

Topographic maps should be used with a compass to determine your location. Although you can supplement topographic maps with national park, national forest, or provincial park maps, only the topographic map, with its contour lines, provides essential information about the lay of the land. Know all the symbols used on topographic maps, and don't wait until you are lost to discover that your orienteering skills aren't up to par. See Appendix C to find some helpful books on map and compass use. If you need to hone your navigational skills, join an orienteering club. Orienteering is a popular sport with a national organization (see Appendix B) and local clubs that hold competitive meets and provide instruction for newcomers. Orienteering can be a good way to spend the warm months while waiting for the snow to come. And when the snow returns, you'll be ready to do your orienteering on snowshoes.

Store maps in a container that will keep them dry. Buy a case specially designed for that purpose, or improvise. You can also coat your maps with a waterproofing chemical so they won't be damaged or destroyed if they get wet.

Altimeters, devices for measuring elevation, are useful for navigation. Knowing your elevation may help you pinpoint your location on a topographic map.

Backcountry navigators now have a new piece of equipment that can help them "stay found." Global Positioning System (GPS) receivers have come down enough in price over the past few years that they are now rea-

sonably affordable. Prices begin at less than $200. These receivers pick up signals from a network of 24 satellites that orbit the earth, and they use these signals to pinpoint your location. The user can store "waypoints" in the GPS device. A snowshoer can, for example, set the trailhead as a waypoint and mark a number of other points along the route as waypoints—like Hansel and Gretel's trail of crumbs. On the return segment of the outing, the GPS device will guide the snowshoer from one waypoint to another and finally back to the trailhead—and no one will have eaten them up, or covered them with snow. This is an excellent piece of equipment to own and to use, but these systems must be used with caution. If the batteries become weak or if the system fails because of internal problems, you could become dangerously lost. If you are in a dense forest, the receiver might not be able to pick up the satellite signals. And, this system could direct you over dangerous terrain. Therefore, don't rely solely on such a system. You must know how to use a map and compass, and you should know where you are on the map at all times.

Finding Companions

Joining an outdoor club is an excellent way to find companions for backcountry trips. Clubs allow you to meet people with the same interests, and most of the larger clubs offer classes and seminars on such subjects as snowshoeing, avalanche safety, winter mountaineering, mountain-oriented first aid, cross-country skiing, use of map and compass, and many other topics. Most programs will have a few indoor sessions on equipment, followed by one or more field trips. Considering the dangers of a backcountry accident, the instruction these organizations provide is cheap insurance. A list of larger outdoor organizations appears in Appendix B. Most have thousands of members and many local chapters.

First-rate mountaineering shops sometimes offer classes, too. Check out the special activities at your local shop. You will profit from the learning experience and you will meet others with similar interests.

Be Prepared

Preparing for backcountry outings involves the same mindset needed for recreational outings, only the potential dangers and discomforts are far greater, demanding that your technical and wilderness survival skills be much more advanced.

Dangers on the Trail

Learn to recognize and avoid dangerous terrain—cornices, avalanche-prone slopes, and avalanche runout zones. Avalanche danger increases as you head into steeper terrain. On more advanced mountaineering trips, crevasses present another danger. You must also be able to recognize when the terrain simply cannot be crossed on snowshoes, and you must know self-arrest procedures in the event of a fall on a steep slope. The technical training acquired through club-sponsored schools can prepare you for backcountry hazards.

Pacing Yourself

Regardless of whether you're on an easy trip or a tough backcountry journey, keep the pace comfortable so that you and your companions don't become exhausted. Use the rest step. In the deep snow and rougher conditions of the backcountry, you must greatly reduce mileage expectations. The heavier gear load will also slow you down. Make sure group members share the task of breaking trail. One way to do this is to have the lead snowshoer step aside after an agreed upon amount of time and fall in at the end of the line. Each person thus takes a turn.

Chapter Seven

Running and Racing

The Sport

Running and racing on snowshoes is not new. Earlier accounts of snowshoeing activities report numerous racing events. The sport was revitalized when runners realized the new breed of high-tech snowshoes could enable them to continue their training runs on snow-covered terrain. Soon manufacturers began offering snowshoes specifically for running on packed trails. As interest in the sport continued to grow, runners began leaving trails and heading into the backcountry. Running on snowshoes now takes place on all types of terrain.

The Aluminum-Frame Racing Snowshoe

Many of the larger manufacturers of high-tech snowshoes offer a model specifically designed for running on packed trails. Typically, these snowshoes are offered in only one size, usually 8 by 25 inches, but because they are designed for use on packed trails, they are suitable for even relatively large runners. Designers of running models use variations of the same basic components that constitute recreational and backcountry snowshoes—frame shape, pivot system, bindings, and traction devices—to craft a snowshoe that meets the specific needs of runners. The overall emphasis is on minimizing weight; you will find models that weigh less than 2 pounds per pair.

Frame Shape

Many manufacturers use an asymmetrical frame because it provides more medial clearance. You will find a number of interesting designs. Yuba's running snowshoe has an asymmetrical frame that resembles the shape of the human foot. Tubbs uses an asymmetrical frame with a cutout section in the rear. Atlas and Sherpa each have a uniquely shaped symmetrical frame.

Some runners are now leaving the trails and heading into deeper snow, and the typical 8 by 25 inch snowshoe does not always provide sufficient flotation, especially for larger runners. Some manufacturers do, however, have models that they recommend for running through deep snow. Yuba offers a larger asymmetrical snowshoe that is suitable for off-trail use; Good Thunder also has one, as does Sherpa; and all of Northern Lites's models are very lightweight and can be used for off-trail running. With the increasing interest in snowshoeing, we may see manufacturers developing snowshoes specifically for off-trail running.

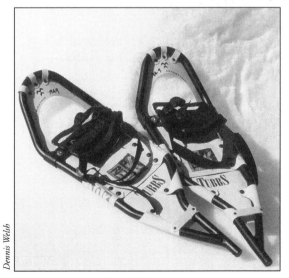

Dennis Welsh

Racing snowshoes from Tubbs.

The Pivot System

Both rotating-pivot and fixed-pivot designs are available. However, many runners, especially those who run on trails, like to have their snowshoes close to their feet, a feature provided by fixed-pivot systems. Most running snowshoes, therefore, use a fixed-pivot strap. Atlas, Redfeather, Tubbs, and Good Thunder use fixed pivots on their running models. Sherpa uses its Dual Rotation system, which allows the pivot rod to be set so that the deck lifts off the ground and reduces the heel slap that occurs with some designs. Yuba uses a rotating-pivot system that allows the deck to rotate approximately 60 degrees.

The Bindings

Bindings must be secure yet easy to get in and out of. Many designers use nylon straps across the toes, another across the instep, and a third to secure the heel. Since many runners wear their regular running shoes, some type of additional insulation is often necessary. Insulated bindings are available from several companies—including Sherpa, Redfeather, and Good Thunder—and the list will probably grow. Yuba has a bootie that fits over running shoes, while some runners use the neoprene booties designed for cycling.

Traction Devices

Smaller traction devices are usually better for runners, at least on snowshoes designed for trail use. With longer devices you have to lift your feet higher off the ground. The smaller devices also save weight. Some manufacturers use titanium traction devices, which are very strong and very lightweight.

Clothing

Like other snowshoers, runners need to layer their clothing. But unlike recreationalists and backcountry users, runners will be burning huge amounts of energy the entire time they're out, even if it's only for an hour or so. Thus, their layering needs are a bit different. The first layer must be capable of moving moisture away from the body, and the second layer must provide insulation and continue transporting moisture away from the body. However, because of all the heat being produced, one layer sometimes provides enough insulation. Some high-tech garment fabrics provide both wicking and insulating proper-

Injection-Molded Snowshoes for the Runner

TSL makes an injection-molded snowshoe platform that supports a binding designed specifically for the runner. This is a rela-tively new snowshoe technology in this country; time will tell if it will make serious inroads into the market.

Dennis Welsh

ties, allowing the runner to use just one moisture-managing layer instead of separate inner and middle layers, especially during warmer weather or times of extreme exertion.

Runners may also need an outer layer. The highly aerobic nature of running requires an outer shell that's very breathable. It is worn when weather conditions—colder temperatures and rain or snow—warrant. Microfiber shells or shells made out of W. L. Gore and Associates' Activent fabric may be the best choices. Both fabrics provide protection from the wind, are highly water-resistant, and are very breathable. However, runners who will be out in very wet weather need breathable

shells that are absolutely waterproof (and breathable), not just water-resistant. In this case, shell garments made out of Gore-Tex are best. Those heading off established trails should make sure they have the proper degree of weather protection.

Head gear is important, as are mittens or gloves. Headbands allow dissipation of some of the huge heat output, while still protecting the ears. Gaiters are necessary, especially if you wear snowshoes that kick up a lot of snow. In fact, you may need to wear an outer shell regularly if your snowshoes tend to coat your legs and back with snow.

Footgear

Superlight footgear complements superlight snowshoes. Many runners use regular running shoes, supplemented by either an insulated binding or a bootie, as already noted. If you are using running shoes, it's a good idea to wear a size that permits you to wear an extra pair of warm socks.

Select footgear suitable for the terrain, weather, snow conditions, and distance you'll be traveling. If you run into the backcountry, wear more substantial footgear, such as lightweight boots. Your footgear must be adequate for any emergency that may delay your return.

What to Bring Along

On a very short run near home, you may be able to get by without a pack. However, the cautious runner will carry a small pack that can hold at least a quart of water and extra clothing, such as an outer shell and a middle insulating layer. A fanny pack or small lumbar pack may be enough for nearby runs. Most of the packs designed for runners have outside insulated hol-

sters for water bottles and a small compartment for gear. They are usually very stable.

Runners heading into the backcountry and climbing peaks benefit from lumbar and torso packs that have internal water storage reservoirs. These carry lots of water, which the runner can drink without having to stop and take off the pack. Their proximity to the body helps keep the water from freezing.

If you want to run any distance into the backcountry, carry a pack large enough to hold the safety essentials (see page 102). The farther you go from the trailhead, the more important the need for emergency gear.

Technique

Running on snowshoes doesn't require a lot of technique, especially on packed trails and fairly level terrain. Runners who venture off trail and into the backcountry should know how to use the hardware on their snowshoes to climb and descend.

Don't plan to run as quickly in snow as you do on dry pavement. Your snowshoes may be lightweight, but even 2 pounds can slow you down. Running in deep snow adds still more difficulty. Of course, even running on trails requires more attention to surface conditions than does running on dry roads. When running competitively, taking a tumble can mean the difference between winning and losing.

Poles are optional. Because they add stability, take them along for deep snow or steep terrain.

Places to Go

Snow-covered roads are a great possibility for runners, as are local parks and golf courses. Runners can use nature or hiking trails or even head into the backcountry. The sport offers many options. Make sure, however, that your footwear, clothing, gear, and expertise are appropriate for the type of run you have in mind.

Locating Races and Other Events

There are plenty of competitive events, many sponsored by the snowshoe manufacturing companies. Tubbs, Sherpa, Atlas, Redfeather, Northern Lites, and Good Thunder all sponsor races. You can locate information about upcoming events in *Snowshoer* magazine (see Appendix C) or contact the manufacturers themselves to ask about events in your area. The addresses and telephone numbers for the snowshoeing companies are in Appendix A. You can also check local winter-sports magazines and organizations for event information.

Part Five

Watching Your Step

Playing It Safe

Against the Elements

Don't become a statistic. Many people die needlessly in the backcountry because they were unprepared for potential health and terrain hazards. Wear clothing suitable for winter travel, carry the necessary gear, know the dangers, and have the good sense to head home if bad weather threatens.

Hypothermia

Sometimes called "exposure," hypothermia develops when the body starts to lose heat faster than it can produce it, and your core temperature begins to drop. This drop is caused by the heat loss mechanisms discussed on pages 73–74. As the body's core temperature begins to fall, a number of physiological events take place as the body tries to conserve heat. These, in turn, translate into a number of observable behaviors that alert you that a companion is in danger of becoming a victim of hypothermia.

The early stages are characterized by shivering, goose bumps, and an inability to perform complex tasks with the hands. The victim is said to be mildly hypothermic when the body temperature drops to 95 degrees Fahrenheit. When the core temperature drops below this point, shivering becomes more intense, the lack of muscular coordination becomes more apparent, and the victim may become confused or have difficulty speaking. In his book on the subject, *The Basic Essentials of Hypothermia,* Dr. William Forgey says that the best field test for mild hypothermia is the inability of the victim to walk a 30-foot straight line.

Once the core temperature drops below 90 degrees Fahrenheit, the victim usually stops shivering because the body does not have enough energy reserves to produce this response. Mental ability deteriorates, and the victim is said to be severely or profoundly hypothermic. As core temperature continues to drop, the muscles become rigid, and pulse and respiration slow. Death can occur when the core temperature reaches approximately 78 degrees.

The observable symptoms of both mild hypothermia and profound hypothermia vary. One of the problems with providing first aid for hypothermia victims, therefore, is that it can be difficult to determine simply on the basis of observation whether a victim is mildly or profoundly hypothermic, a crucial distinction. In all cases, however, first aid starts with preventing further heat loss. Shelter the victim from the wind, replace wet clothing, and add layers of insulation. Beyond that, however, treatment differs. For the mildly hypothermic victim, external heat sources, such as hot water bottles or chemical heat-generating pads, may be used to restore warmth. The victim also may be given warm beverages and food. For the severely hypothermic victim, a main requirement after preventing further heat loss is to handle the victim gently, since the heart is very sensitive to cold. Abrupt movement can cause ventricular fibrillation. Rewarming a profoundly hypothermic victim is best done in a hospital under controlled conditions. Since this is not always possible, field warming can be done, but it is a complex subject that is best learned in a mountain-oriented first aid course. Learn as much as you can about hypothermia and its symptoms. Even if you and your group take adequate precautions against it, you may come upon a victim who needs first aid. It is very important to remember that hypothermia can also develop during the summer. All it takes is an unprepared hiker who gets soaked by a cold rain and further cooled by high winds far from the trailhead.

It's worth noting again: Remember to eat well when you're snowshoeing; you'll need significantly more calories than usual. Drink lots of water; the body requires it for proper energy production.

Frostbite

Despite its innocent-sounding name, frostbite can be a serious, painful, and even crippling condition. Here's a condensation of what wilderness medicine expert Dr. Paul G. Gill, Jr., has to say, in his *Ragged Mountain Press Guide to Wilderness Medicine & First-Aid* (see Appendix C), about frostbite and its prevention and treatment:

Frostbite is tissue injury or death caused by exposure to subfreezing cold, and it can be broken into three stages. *Frostnip*, the body's first response to freezing temperatures, involves stinging pain, numbness, and blanched skin. It looks like a small white patch, usually on the cheeks, nose, or ears.

Ignore frostnip and it will progress to the *superficial* stage: the skin becomes pale or gray and cold to the touch. A day or so later, blisters will form. *Deep frostbite* involves deep freezing of tissues. The injured part is purple or red, cool to the touch, and void of sensation. Small blood blisters will form after one or two weeks, and the part might remain swollen for months. Eventually it will mummify and fall off.

You can treat *frostnipped* hands anywhere, anytime, Dr. Gill notes, by breathing through cupped hands or putting your hands in your armpits. "But there's a time and a place for the treatment of frostbite," Dr. Gill adds. "The place is *indoors* and the time is when you're sure that there's no chance that the thawed part will be refrozen."

Dr. Gill continues: "Start thawing the injured part as soon as you get to secure shelter. The key to recovery from frostbite is *rapid rewarming*. Fill a large container with water heated to between 104°F to 108°F (40°C to

Paul Svetlik

Mountaineering First Aid

In everyday circumstances, a standard American Red Cross first-aid course will prepare you for many medical emergencies and give you enough information to treat an injury until the ambulance arrives. But calling 911 isn't often an option for those of us who head to the mountains and forests. If an accident occurs or an illness strikes, help is usually hours and sometimes days away.

Wilderness trekkers need advanced first-aid training, and some mountaineers and medical professionals have given careful thought to the first-aid skills needed in the backcountry. In 1968, the Mountaineers—a nonprofit outdoor activity and conservation club—in conjunction with the American Red Cross, put together a Mountaineering Oriented First-Aid (MOFA) class that included information on the skills and essential gear a backcountry traveler needs to prevent accidents and injuries. (Many MOFA classes use *Mountaineering First-Aid*, published by the Mountaineers, as their textbook.)

Larger mountain clubs usually offer MOFA classes. Take the course if you can. If a mountain club class is not available, check the bulletin board at your local mountaineering shop.

42°C) and immerse the frostbitten area in it. Make sure you remove all jewelry and constrictive clothing and don't allow the [body] part to rest on the bottom or sides of the vessel."

Dr. Gill recommends continuing the rewarming until the victim's skin becomes soft and flushed, which should take no more than 30 minutes. When finished, gently dry the affected part with a clean towel, place sterile gauze or cotton between fingers and toes, and apply aloe vera or antibiotic ointment to the damaged skin.

The best way to beat frostbite is not to get it in the first place. Here are some of Dr. Gill's tips on preventing frostbite:

- Eat well before a trip, and avoid alcohol and tobacco
- Avoid tight clothing and boots
- Keep your head, neck, and face covered
- Never touch metal with bare hands
- Keep fingernails and toenails trimmed

Sunburn

The "safety essentials" include sun protection. Not only do the sun's rays beat down on you from above, they also reflect back up to you off the snow below. Even on a cloudy day you can get sunburned. Apply sunscreen to all exposed parts of your body before you start your trip. A hat with a brim provides additional protection.

Snowblindness

The sun can burn the surface of the eyes, causing snowblindness. Symptoms often do not develop until several hours after exposure. In most cases, the eyes feel dry and irritated, but in more severe cases you may experience difficulty seeing and severe pain. The condition usually resolves itself, but its long-term effects are unclear. To prevent snowblindness, wear sunglasses or tinted goggles that absorb at least 80 percent of the visible light and 90 percent of the ultraviolet radiation.

Other Medical Problems

Almost any medical emergency that can develop at home can also occur in the back-country. A knowledge of first aid in general, and mountain-oriented first aid in particular, are important. If the local chapter of an outdoor club offers a mountaineering first aid course, take it. You will find suggestions for additional reading on wilderness first aid in Appendix C.

Avalanches

A beautiful mountain covered with glistening snow can become deadly when the right combination of terrain and snow conditions leads to an avalanche. Colorado has the dubious honor of leading the United States in avalanche deaths, but many fatalities also occur in Washington, Alaska, and other mountainous states, and in the mountainous provinces in Canada.

Loose Snow Avalanches

Loose snow avalanches start when gravity or another force causes a few snow grains to begin tumbling down a slope. The sliding snow usually spreads out laterally as the moving grains dislodge other grains, eventually forming an inverted-V pattern as the avalanche grows. Loose snow avalanches generally do not bring down a lot of snow.

Slab Avalanches

A slab avalanche is much more dramatic and much more deadly than a loose snow avalanche. The slab avalanche is a cohesive layer of snow that breaks loose and comes thundering down the mountainside, taking everything in its path on a deadly ride and burying all those who were not able to escape. The fracture line where the slab breaks loose is usually high up on the slope. After it comes down the slope, sometimes at very high speeds, it reaches level ground, called the runout zone, and comes to a stop. Once buried in such a slide, the victim's only hope of survival is a quick rescue by companions.

What Causes a Slab Avalanche?

A basic factor contributing to the formation of slab avalanches is the layered structure of the snowpack. Each snowstorm adds a new layer. After the snow falls, the newly deposited layer settles under its own weight, forming a cohesive layer. A number of weather events can subsequently occur that influence the probability of future avalanches.

Before we look at those events, let's first consider the essential elements that must be present to have a slab avalanche. These are a slope, a cohesive layer or slab of snow, a weak layer within the snowpack that does not bond well to the layer above it, and a trigger. That's all it takes. With gravity constantly pulling the snow downward, the trigger simply upsets the delicate bond holding the snowpack onto that weak layer. That trigger can be any number of things. It can be the added stress caused by the weight of a new layer of snow. Or, it can be the additional weight of a snowshoer on the slope. The trigger causes a fracture, and the slab slides off of the layer to which it was weakly bonded. The outcome is that awe-inspiring mass of snow that tears down the mountain.

What produces that weak layer? Actually, it varies. In some parts of the country, weather conditions change the snow crystals within the snowpack, forming a type of crystal that does not bond well to the layer above. These newly formed crystals, sometimes referred to as "sugar snow" or "depth hoar," form weak layers in the snowpack. Weather conditions in Colorado are perfect for the formation of these weak layers, which is probably why Colorado has experienced so many avalanche deaths.

A number of other conditions can produce weak layers. Hoar frost, the wintertime equivalent of dew, can do it. Hoar frost forms beautiful, feathery crystals on top of the snow. When they become buried by the next snowfall, they, too, create a weak layer in the snowpack. A rainstorm followed by cold weather can produce a slick surface off of which a slab produced by the next snowstorm can slide. Meltwater can also contribute to the development of an avalanche. As it percolates down through the layers, it can destroy bonds between layers, again setting the stage for an avalanche. Many other conditions can lead to the formation of avalanches. It is important that you know the weather conditions that are the primary causes of avalanches in the mountains where you will snowshoe.

Staying Out of Harm's Way

Snowshoers can reduce avalanche danger by learning how to recognize avalanche terrain, how to evaluate the stability of the snowpack, and how to select a safe route. If you snowshoe in avalanche-prone areas, learn about and carry avalanche safety and rescue equipment, and learn about and practice avalanche rescue procedures. These subjects could fill a whole book or course of study. The guidelines that follow will touch only briefly on these subjects, to alert you to the kind of study and the type of training you need to travel safely through avalanche country.

Route Selection

Most slab avalanches occur on slopes with angles between 30 and 45 degrees. Most naturally releasing avalanches occur during or immediately after either a snowstorm or a windstorm that transports snow. This occurs because, as noted above, the extra weight of the new layer of snow provides the final stress needed to break the bond between the weak layer and the slab above it. When traveling in avalanche country, observe the following guidelines to maximize your safety:

- Even after high danger periods have passed, select routes that take you along wide valley floors, away from steep slopes.

- Don't stop for lunch or a rest stop in any area that might be a runout zone for an avalanche slope.

- If you must cross a slope, remember that your weight could trigger an avalanche; cross on the ridge above the slope.

- Stay away from cornices; don't stand on them, near them, or below them.

- Stay out of steep bowls and gullies.
- Be suspicious of a gentle slope if there is a steep slope above it.
- Never traverse a steep slope unless you are sure that it is stable.
- If you need to ascend, try to do so in areas of dense timber. Don't be fooled into thinking that a few trees will anchor the snow.

Those who elect to risk snowshoeing on or across slopes in avalanche terrain must learn how to evaluate the stability of a slope. One method is to dig a snow pit in a safe place near the slope being evaluated. The pit exposes the layered structure of the snowpack so that several tests can be performed to determine how strong the bond is between the layers. Describing these tests is beyond the scope of this book, but you can refer to the resources listed in Appendix C to learn more.

If You're Caught

If you are caught in an avalanche, you have a split second to try to escape to the side, if possible, or grab a tree or anything that will keep you from becoming part of the moving mass of snow. If you are carried off, shout to alert your friends; then keep your mouth closed so you won't inhale a mouthful of snow. If possible, try to discard as much of your heavy equipment as you can. The goal is to ditch equipment that will drag you down. Snowshoers, unfortunately, cannot ditch their snowshoes, but they can get rid of their poles. Try to stay near the surface of the mass of moving snow so you won't be totally buried when the avalanche comes to a stop. Making swimming motions will help you do that if you are upright as you are being swept down the slope. When you feel the snow coming to a stop, try to make an air pocket in front of your face.

Kathy Horiuchi

The aftermath of a slab avalanche.

Safety Equipment

An avalanche shovel is essential. These are lightweight and usually have a telescoping or removable handle. They can be used to dig snow pits for stability evaluations or to dig out an avalanche victim. Some backcountry packs have a special pocket for storing an avalanche shovel. Collapsible probe poles, light and easy to carry, can be extended to 8 to 10 feet to be used to help find a buried victim.

Avalanche beacons offer the victim the greatest chance of being found quickly. These small electronic devices, sometimes called transceivers, emit and receive a radio signal. Each member of the group should have one. Here is how they're used. After a stability evaluation has been performed and the decision to travel on the slope has been made, group members enter the slope one at a time. The transceivers of all group members are set to "transmit." As one member enters the slope, the remaining members watch the person the entire time he or she is on the slope. If the slope avalanches, members note the point where they last saw the victim. When the avalanche stops, the group makes sure the slope is safe to enter, turns their avalanche beacons to "receive," and begins the search. While effective use of beacons provides the greatest hope for a quick location, some practice and skill is needed to use them.

Unfortunately, some transceivers operate on 2275 Hz. Others use 457 kHz. The 457 kHz signal has been found to be superior, and beginning January 1, 1996, only beacons transmitting on the 457 kHz frequency were being sold in the United States. While the

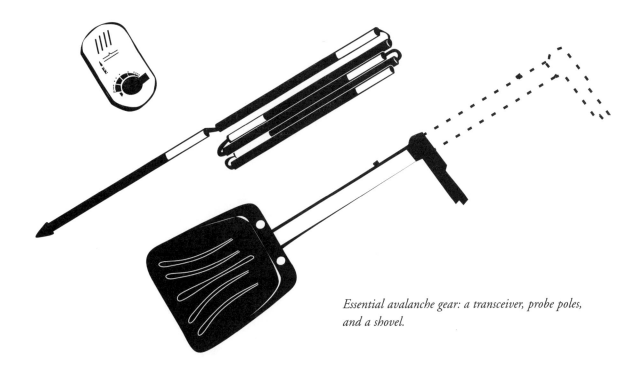

Essential avalanche gear: a transceiver, probe poles, and a shovel.

2275 Hz frequency is being phased out, units using this frequency are still around, as are units that use both frequencies. Make sure all group members have beacons that send and receive on the same frequency.

In most types of accidents, someone is immediately sent for help. This is not wise with avalanche accidents since the surviving group members provide the victim's best hope for a quick rescue. Assuming the victim was not killed by being battered against rocks and trees while the avalanche was moving, the probability of a live recovery drops to 50 percent after 30 minutes. Unless additional help is nearby, use all available group members to search for the victim. By the time a rescue party arrives, the victim will probably have suffocated.

Snowshoes on Annapurna IV

In September 1996, we arrived in Katmandu, Nepal, for the Annapurna IV 1996 Memory Climb. The team first flew north to an airstrip located near the Tibetan border, and, from there, donkeys carried our nearly two tons of equipment (including three pairs of snowshoes from one of our sponsors, Sherpa, Inc.) up the mountain to our Base Camp at 16,000 feet. We made excellent progress up the mountain to Camp 1 at 18,000 feet, when, on the morning of October 4, tragedy struck. A snowstorm of unexpected intensity had begun the previous evening and left three meters of snow over the next 36 hours. Two of the three people weathering out the storm at Camp 1— Debbie Marshal and Rich Davidson—died from asphyxiation when snow covered up their tent's ventilation openings. The rest of us who had descended to Base Camp before the storm were unharmed.

The snow accumulation was so great that, for the person stranded at Camp 1, descending the fixed line to Base Camp would have been certain death. The only remaining option was to request that the Nepalese Army evacuate him by helicopter. I sent a sherpa down on foot to a nearby police checkpoint to radio for help. He returned an hour later, turned back by shoulder-deep drifts several hundred yards from camp. We outfitted him with a pair of snowshoes and briefly instructed him on how to use them. He struck out again late in the afternoon. We learned of his success early the following morning when the helicopter arrived. The sherpa had flown up to show the pilot our camp. The pilot was barely able to rescue the stranded climber and then flew him to Katmandu for medical observation.

The rest of us remained in Base Camp for a week until the snow consolidated and we were able to ascend to Camp 1. We wore snowshoes all the way up to the higher camp and spent three days bringing down equipment and the two bodies. We buried our friends at Base Camp in accordance with their wishes and with climbing tradition.

Chad Alber
Leader, Annapurna IV
1996 Memory Climb

Shocking, But True

Never underestimate the possibility of a lightning strike.

When I first got to Colorado, I started climbing some of the "14ers"—peaks over 14,000 feet. One of those early climbs, up Quandary Peak, taught me a lesson I won't forget.

The climb was uneventful, celebrated with lunch at the top. As I started down, I noticed storms moving in. As a relative newcomer, I wasn't concerned at the sight. After all, it wasn't raining on the mountain, and I didn't see any lightning.

Though it was summer in the valley below, I was still way above the timberline and wearing a winter hat. Suddenly, my head started to buzz— a strange sensation, to say the least. I heard a friend shout and turned to see everyone nearby on the ground. Still standing, I had become the local lightning rod. I rolled to the ground, and the buzzing stopped. Someone motioned to me to get into a nearby depression, but as I stood a lightning bolt struck, seemingly right next to me. Frightened, I dove to the side to avoid it.

Then I panicked. I tossed my aluminum-frame pack, with all my raingear, over the side of the mountain. Then it began to hail. A kindly stranger shared his poncho with me as I slithered by along the rocks, too frightened to get up.

Within 10 minutes the storm was over and the sun was shining again. I was even able to retrieve my pack. I was, however, forever changed. I now had a new respect for the power of nature, and a realization that I had been nearly wiped out. The "buzzing" was electricity bouncing off my head. Were it not for my hat, my hair would have stood up straight, and I would have recognized that as a danger signal. I was lucky to have survived, suffering nothing more than a severe case of fear and panic.

Living in Avalanche Country

Learn about safe winter travel, how to select safe routes, and how to analyze the stability of the snowpack. Many victims die because they did not recognize the danger.

It does not take a huge avalanche to kill you. Although films of massive avalanches thundering down the mountainside are impressive, most victims die on relatively short slopes of less than 300 feet.

At a national park, national forest, or a state or provincial park, check with the ranger to see if your planned route presents any avalanche hazard. There may also be a local hot line for the latest weather and avalanche conditions. Take an avalanche awareness class; if you live in avalanche prone areas, training is often available at a reasonable cost from a local mountain club, outdoor organization, or mountaineering shop. Try to take a class that has an outdoor session in which you learn to dig snow pits and evaluate the snow layers.

Overall, when you head into the mountains in the winter, never exceed the level of your stamina, expertise, or equipment.

Electrical Storms

Electrical storms can occur in the winter and are very dangerous above treeline, where the snowshoer is frequently the tallest object around. If an electrical storm is moving in, try to head for lower ground. You are safer in the forest than you are above timberline. However, avoid standing under isolated trees or isolated groups of trees. Open meadows are often dan-gerous. If you cannot get to a sheltered place, and if you feel your skin tingle or your hair standing up straight, you are in very serious danger; squat down and try to lower your pro-file. Do not lie on the ground, however, because this can allow elec-trical current from a nearby strike to travel through your body.

Other Hazards

When planning a trip, study a topographic map for the location of lakes, swampy areas, and streams—important because a frozen lake may look like a meadow after it is covered with snow. Is it safe to snowshoe across the lake, or would it be safer to travel around it? Stream crossings present another danger. How can you determine if a snow bridge covering a stream is safe?

Unfortunately, you won't find any easy answers to such questions. Knowledge of weather patterns in the area helps. If you are in a national or state park, local officials may be able to provide some guidance. Beyond that, you are traveling at risk. Before you cross any body of water, evaluate the conse-quences of falling through. If you're in a marshy area, falling through may amount to getting wet, which makes you vulnerable to hypothermia. If you fall through the ice on a lake, however, you might easily drown. Simi-larly, if you cross a stream on a snow bridge and it breaks through, you might be washed under the snow cover. These are realities you must consider before you take the risk. If you do decide to cross, remember that rising tem-peratures during the day may weaken the snow or ice enough that you cannot cross it safely on your return.

Whiteouts caused by blowing snow pre-sent another backcountry danger, as do low cloud ceilings and fog. All limit visibility, requiring navigation with a map and com-pass. In fact, once you leave the more familiar snow-covered roads and well-defined trails, always keep track of exactly where you are on a map, so that you can find the way back in case bad weather suddenly moves in and obscures visual cues. Don't plan on returning by following your tracks in the snow; wind and blowing snow can quickly cover them. Also, pay attention to the time and how much daylight remains so that you can be back at the trailhead before it gets dark.

Winter travel is serious business, but it can be done safely. Backcountry snowshoeing requires good navigation skills, an ability to evaluate avalanche conditions, proper clothing and gear to deal with emergency bivouacs, and the common sense to abort the trip if weather worsens. Give safety top priority so that you and your companions will arrive home safely, ready to plan your next snowshoeing trip.

Dennis Welsh

APPENDIX A:
Snowshoe
Manufacturers

Modern Snowshoe Manufacturers

Listed below, in alphabetical order, are companies that make high-tech snowshoes. Some of them are small companies, recent entrants into the market, selling only a few hundred pairs, while others are larger, selling thousands of pairs. You will find a brief comment about each company's products, just enough to make you curious and make you want to get their brochure. The comments are by no means inclusive of all that the company offers.

In addition to snowshoes, many companies carry accessories like snowpoles, booties, special binding packages to assist with transitioning between sports, and much more. Some companies make specific models for recreational snowshoers and specific models for backcountry snowshoers. Others offer designs that function under a wide range of conditions. You need to review a company's brochure to find out all that they offer.

Atlas Snowshoes

Atlas was the first company to make heel traction devices standard on all their snowshoes. Their backcountry models uses a unique adaptation of the fixed-pivot system that is called a "Spring Loaded Binding."

Atlas Snowshoe Company
1830 Harrison St.
San Francisco, CA 94103
(800) 645-SHOE

Boldas Snowshoes

Offers injection-molded snowshoes that are made in France.

Boldas Snowshoes
Vanguard Development International, Inc.
1660 17th Street, Suite 110
Denver, CO 80202
(303)607-9498

Elfman Snowshoes

Elfman snowshoes fold to fit into a small pack.

Elfman Snowshoes
245 Tank Farm Road, Unit K
San Luis Obispo, CA 93401
(805) 543-2822

Good Thunder Snowshoes

Good Thunder offers many models, and they offer most of their frame sizes in both symmetrical and asymmetrical designs.

Good Thunder Sports, Inc.
3945 Aldrich Avenue South
Minneapolis, MN 55409
(612) 824-2385

Havlick Snowshoes

Havlick Snowshoes have a unique "Trail Tail" which serves as a backward slide break and saves the tail from wear and tear. They also offer a line of traditional wooden snowshoes.

Havlick Snowshoe Company
2513 State Highway 30, Drawer QQ
Mayfield, New York 12117
(800) TOP-SHOE

Indian Summer Snowshoes

These snowshoes are made by Sherpa and are are targeted to the occasional user.

Sherpa Snowshoe Company
444 South Pine Street
Burlington, WI
(800) 621-2277

Mountain Climber Snowshoes

Offers mountaineering snowshoes with step-in bindings.

Mountain Climber Snowshoes
c/o SP Company, 7482 Cranell Drive
Boulder, CO 80303
(303) 494-1300

MSR Snowshoes

MSR offers a modular injection-molded snowshoe. The basic snowshoe is 22 inches long. The length can be extended with an additional "flotation tail," available in two sizes.

Mountain Safety Research
P. O. Box 24547
Seattle, WA 98124
(800) 877-9677

Northern Lites Snowshoes

Northern Lites made snowshoe weight a major issue. As a result, their snowshoes do weigh less than most other comparably sized recreational and backcountry snowshoes.

Northern Lites
1300 Cleveland
Wausau, WI 55401
(800) 360-LITE

Permagrin Snowshoes

Permagrin offers symmetrical frame snowshoes with an asymmetrical binding that is shaped like the human foot.

Permagrin Adventure Products
P. O. Box 1075
Vail, CO 81658
(970) 949-1143

Polarpaws

Polarpaws are made out of aircraft aluminum. The frames have serrated edges to provide lateral traction.

Polar Equipment Company
12881 Foothill Lane
Saratoga, CA 95070
(408) 867-4576

Powder Wings

Powder Wings offers compactible snowshoes that, when compacted, fit into a fanny pack.

Wing Enterprises, Inc.
P. O. Box 3100
Springville, UT 84663
(800) 453-1192

Redfeather Snowshoes

Redfeather pioneered the use of the V-tail frame with aluminum snowshoes. They offer a large number of snowshoes using the V-tail frame and they offer an injection-molded folding snowshoe.

Redfeather Designs, Inc.
4955 Peoria Street
Denver, CO 80239
(800) 525-0081

Romp Snowshoes

Romp uses a uniquely shaped asymmetrical frame.

Romp Snowshoes
121 S. Robinson
Florence, CO 81226
(800) 324-4162

Sherpa Snowshoes

Sherpa offers a large line of snowshoes and different binding options. They have also introduced Dual Rotation, a system that combines the best features of rotating- and fixed-pivot systems.

Sherpa Snowshoe Company:
444 South Pine Street
Burlington, WI 53105
(800) 621-2277

Sno Trekker Snowshoes

These snowshoes pull apart and snap-together and are designed to serve as an emergency road shovel.

Sno Trekker Snowshoes
C. S. M. Inc.
6730 Springhill Road
Belgrade, MT 59714
(800) 238-3920

TSL Snowshoes

TSL offers injection-molded snowshoes that are made in France and sold around the world.

TSL Snowshoes
925 NW 19th, Suite A
Portland, OR 97209
(503)241-9380

Tubbs Snowshoes

Tubbs offers many different models, all of which, except their running model, use symmetrical frames. They also offer a traditional wood-frame snowshoe with the high-tech binding that they have on their backcountry model.

Tubbs Snowshoe Company
52 River Road, P.O. Box 207
Stowe, VT 05672
(800)-882-2748

Yuba Snowshoes

Yuba offers an asymmetrical frame that is shaped like the human foot.

Yuba Shoes Sport Snowshoes
161 Main Ave.
Sacramento, CA 95838
(800) 598-YUBA

Traditional Wood-Frame Snowshoes

Faber Snowshoes

180, boul. de la Riviere
C. P. 100 Loretteville
Quebec, Canada G2B 3W
(418) 842-8476

Faber offers a large selection of frame designs and has wood-frame models to which new technologies have been applied.

Great Canadian Snowshoes

Great Canadian Canoe Co.
Route 146
Sutton, MA 01590
(800)98-CANOE

Iverson Snowshoes

P. O. Box 85
Shingleton, MI 49884
(906) 452-6370

Wilcox and Williams, Inc.

6105 Halifax Avenue
Edina, MN 55424
(800)216-0710

The company sells both kits and finished snowshoes.

The following companies that are listed with manufacturers of high-tech snowshoes also offer traditional wood-frame snowshoes:

Havlick Snowshoes
Tubbs Snowshoe Company

Unhinged Snowshoes

Spring Brook Mfg., Inc

2477 I Road
Grand Junction, CO 81505
(970) 241-8546

This company sells an unhinged variety called Little Bear Snowshoes.

Mukluks

Steger Mukluks offers many styles and has a good mail-order catalog. Its mukluks have been used on expeditions to the North and South Poles.

Steger Mukluks, Inc.
125 North Central
Ely, MN 55731
(800) MUK-LUKS (685-5857)

You can find a list of private individuals who make mukluks in Garrett and Alexandra Conover's *A Snow Walker's Companion,* published by Ragged Mountain Press in 1995 (see Appendix C). The book also lists the names and addresses of companies that manufacture and sell fine woolen clothing.

APPENDIX B:
Hiking and
Outdoor Clubs

The following hiking and outdoor clubs have large memberships. Contact them for a listing of their local chapters and for general membership information.

Adirondack Mountain Club
814 Goggins Road
Lake George, NY 12845
(518) 668-4447

Appalachian Mountain Club
5 Joy Street
Boston, MA 02108
(617) 523-0636

Colorado Mountain Club
710 10th Street
Golden, CO 80401
(303) 279-3080

Green Mountain Club
Route 100
RR 1 Box 650
Waterbury Center, VT 05677
(802) 244-7037

The Mountaineers
300 Third Avenue West
Seattle, WA 98119
(206) 284-6310

The Sierra Club
730 Polk Street
San Francisco, CA 94109

To locate smaller clubs in your state, contact the American Hiking Society:

American Hiking Society
P O Box 20160
Washington, D. C. 20041

Orienteering Clubs

To locate one in your area contact:

U.S. Orienteering Federation
P.O. Box 1444
Forest Park, GA 30051

APPENDIX C:
Resources:
Books, Videos

Further reading

Snowshoeing

Conover, Garrett and Alexandra. *A Snow Walker's Companion.* Camden, ME: Ragged Mountain Press, 1995.

Gilpatrick, Gil. *Building Snowshoes,* 1996. This book can be ordered directly from the author: Gil Gilpatrick, P.O. Box 461, Skowhegan, Maine 04976

Osgood, William, and Leslie Hurley. *The Snowshoe Book,* 2nd ed. Brattleboro, VT: The Stephen Greene Press, 1975.

Prater, Gene. *Snowshoeing,* 3rd ed. Seattle, WA: The Mountaineers, 1988.

Vaillancourt, Henri. *Making the Attikamek Snowshoe.* Greenville, NH: The Trust for Native American Cultures and Crafts, 1987.

Wilderness Skills

Armstrong, Betsy R., and Knox Williams. *The Avalanche Book.* Golden, CO: Fulcrum Publishing, 1992.

Flemming, June. *Staying Found.* Seattle: The Mountaineers, 1994.

Fredston Jill, and Doug Fesler, *Snow Sense.* Anchorage: Alaska Mountain Safety Center, 1994.

Kjellstrom, Bjorn. *Be Expert with Map & Compass.* New York: Charles Scribner's Sons, 1994.

Meyer, Kathleen. *How to shit in the woods.* Berkeley, CA: Ten Speed Press, 1994.

Seidman, David. *Essential Wilderness Navigator.* Camden, ME: Ragged Mountain Press, 1995

Tawrell, Paul. *Camping and Wilderness Survival.* 1996. (To order, call Upper Access Books, Hinesburg, VT, 1-800-356-9315.)

The Ten Essentials for Travel in the Outdoors. Seattle: The Mountaineers, 1993.

Wilkinson, Ernest. *Snow Caves for Fun and Survival.* Boulder, CO: Johnson Books, 1992.

First Aid

Brown, Robert E. *Emergency/Survival Handbook.* American Outdoor Safety League, 1990.

Carline, Jan D., Ph.D., Martha J. Lentz, R.N., Ph.D., and Steven C. Macdonald, M.P.H., Ph.D. *Mountaineering First Aid,* 4th ed., Seattle: The Mountaineers, 1996.

First Aid, Quick Information for Mountaineering and Backcountry Use. Seattle: The Mountaineers, 1995.

Gill, Paul, MD. *Ragged Mountain Press Guide to Wilderness Medicine & First-Aid.* Camden, ME: Ragged Mountain Press, 1997.

Kennedy, Barbara, M.D. *Caring for Children in the Outdoors.* Adventure Medical Kits, 1994.

Schimelpfenig, Tod, and Linda Lindsey, *NOLS Wilderness First Aid.* Mechanicsburg, PA: The National Outdoor Leadership School and Stackpole Books, 1991.

Tilton, Buck. *Backcountry First Aid and Extended Care.* Merrillville, IN: ICS Books, 1994.

Weiss, Eric A., M.D. *A Comprehensive Guide to Wilderness and Travel Medicine.* Adventure Medical Kits, 1994.

Videos

"Avalanche Awareness, A Question of Balance." Produced by Alliance Communications, Denver, CO. Many outdoor shops sell this videotape, which runs approximately 30 minutes and is an excellent introduction to this deadly phenomenon.

"Finding Your Way in the Wild," available from Quality Video, Inc., 7399 Bush Lake Road, Minneapolis, MN 55439.

"Snow Caves or How to Keep Warm with Ice," available from Vernal Productions, 9 Driftwood Avenue, Novato, CA 94945, (415) 892-2387

Magazines

Snowshoer
P. O. Box 458
Washburn, WI 54891
(715) 373-5556

Backpacker
33 E. Minor Street
Emmaus, PA 18098
(610) 967-5171

Outside
P.O. Box 54729
Boulder, CO 80322
(800) 678-1131
(303) 604-1464 in Colorado

Index

Index